MY MOTHER
AND I

MARGARET POWELL

My Mother
and I

London
MICHAEL JOSEPH

First published in Great Britain in 1972
by Michael Joseph Ltd
52 Bedford Square, London, W.C.1

© 1972 by Margaret Powell and Leigh Crutchley

7181 1043 9

Printed in Great Britain by
Richard Clay (The Chaucer Press) Ltd
Bungay, Suffolk

Chapter One

Mum was born in 1880 out of wedlock. How old-fashioned that phrase, 'out of wedlock', sounds today, when illegitimacy has become a commonplace, but in 1880 to become an unmarried mother was the most awful fate that could befall a woman since it followed on that fate worse than death—the loss of her virginity outside the marriage bed. Nothing was done to comfort the girl, or to make her ordeal easy. Her suffering and the suffering of the child was supposed to cleanse her sin. The man was never blamed. It was considered inherent in a man's nature that he should take his pleasures when and where he could. It was up to the woman to make sure that they were withheld until the right time and the right place—marriage and the marriage bed.

These were Victorian times and for this attitude I reckon Queen Victoria must take most of the blame, because in those days social and moral behaviour was still dictated by the example of the Crown, and Victoria was a very, very respectable woman. I have never been able to imagine her doing anything in wedlock, let alone out of it. From the portraits and photos I've seen she looks so forbidding that the thought of her ever getting into bed with a man seemed to me to be remote. I used to think she slept in her clothes and in a high-backed chair. Yet she did have a lot of children and she was supposed to have loved her husband, but love and sex didn't seem to go hand in hand in those days and, let's face it, for a lot of women it didn't until recent years. No end of women of my generation thought that sex was just their duty to their husbands. They hated it. If they got a husband who wanted sex more than once a week they thought it was shocking. It was a lot to do with the men who hadn't any idea how to make it enjoyable. Selfish beasts men have been and would be now if women hadn't gone for their rights. It was the fault of religion, too, going on about the 'sinful lusts of the flesh'. Talk about trying to take the gilt off the gingerbread!

Although my mother was illegitimate she didn't know it until she was fifteen. She was brought up by her mother's married sister and her husband whom she called 'mother' and 'father'. They had four sons whom she thought of as her brothers. This 'adoption' was not done out of love or even duty by the putative parents but because the disgrace of having a sister with an illegitimate baby was worse than bringing up somebody else's child.

Despite not knowing she was illegitimate, mother was made to suffer and feel unwanted. The sins of her mother were very much visited on her. People automatically hated illegitimate children. She was made 'whipping boy' for every situation that happened in the home. Any mishaps, any accident or any misbehaviour on the part of her brothers was always her fault. She was abused, chastised and ridiculed. Made to do all the menial tasks around the house and even the smallest mistake led to a thrashing. She had to be kept away from school repeatedly until her bruises had faded. It was perhaps as well for her that things got worse so that eventually the neighbours told the police what was going on. Mum got to know this from friends at school. For that to have happened at that time must have meant that she was being treated like a dog. People never went to the police—to inform on your neighbours was treachery of the worst kind. They must have been afraid for my mother's life to have done it. Physically things improved after that but the mental cruelty continued. That mum's spirit wasn't broken at this time is something that has always surprised me. Looking and listening to her now at ninety-one, I think the reverse happened; the punishment and ridicule hardened her determination to survive.

The only relief mum had from this day by day wretchedness came once a month when she was visited by her 'aunt', her real mother. There was a feeling of warmth that came with her and she gave her her first sense of being loved. Mum particularly remembers the day when she felt her own love for someone else stirring—it was the day she got her first present. Her mother came to pay her monthly visit. She went upstairs to mum's room and gave her a large paper parcel. Together they unwrapped it, took the lid off the box and there to mum's great joy and delight was a china doll all dressed up in things her mother had made for it. It was her first real possession and it brought with it the happiest moment in her life: something to love given to her by the only person who had ever shown her love. They played with it together for a few moments then her mother lifted mum up, with the doll clasped tightly to her to carry her downstairs. As they were going down her mother stumbled, reached for the bannister, and as she did so knocked the doll out of mum's hands to fall down the stairs and break its china face on the tiles at the bottom. For both it was a deep human tragedy and mum wept bitter tears as they tried putting the pieces together. Quickly her aunt was on the scene, saw what she thought had happened, that my mum had dropped the doll herself, berated her for it and sent her upstairs to her bedroom. Mum says she's a bit vague about what happened afterwards—she knows she lay sobbing on the bed, and she remembers hearing her aunt and her mother having words downstairs. It must have been several hours later that she woke to see her mother with an identical doll in her arms. She handed it to her, kissed her goodnight and left. As mum says she must have gone all the way back to Brighton, bought another doll, dressed it and come back to Shoreham with it. Apart from the effort of it all there was the money—and all for her. Not that she got much more joy out of it. She went to sleep with the doll in her arms but when she woke the next morning it was gone. Her aunt had taken it. When she asked where it was she was told it was put into safe keeping, 'No point in letting you play with it you'll only break it as you did the other one. I've put it away and you'll only get it when I'm around to see it comes to no harm.'

Mum does remember being given it once or twice on special occasions but as she says a doll is for playing with, loving and talking to when no one else is around, not just something to sit with in your arms for other people to admire.

But like so many people mum was inconsistent. As I reminded her when she told me the story, she used to put our good presents away when we were children. I remember this because as I was fond of reading I was given a lot of books but I was continually losing the thread of stories because I could only have them on certain occasions. Often this was when people came to visit so that I'd sit and be quiet, but of course although I wanted to read I also wanted to listen to what was being said and I could never make up my mind what I really did want to concentrate on.

Since life in her home was so wretched mum spent as much time as she could out of it. So did her 'brothers'. They at least were kind to her, as kind that is as brothers are to a sister or sisters. Shoreham at that time was more a village than a town. It was a pretty sleepy little place dominated some mile or so away by Lancing College. 'Proper lot of toffs they were,' says mum. 'Never had any time for us or for any of the village children. Never noticed us or passed words with us.' I thought that some of them might have flirted with the village girls as Flashman did in *Tom Brown's Schooldays*. 'Never,' said mum. 'It was a school which was founded on religion. Those kind of boys would never think about that sort of thing.' I must say my experience when I was charring for reverend gentlemen has led me to believe differently. Talk about the dignity of the cloth. When one particular vicar used to get me alone I had to thrash about me with a dish cloth to keep his hands off me. In any case I'd have thought that if these boys were going to have to lead a devout life they'd have put in a bit of early overtime for what they were going to miss later. Mind you I've only got mum's word for it, but she's beady-eyed even at ninety-one and never misses a thing, so perhaps she's right.

All around the village were farms and fields and the river was empty except for a few fishing boats. Now of course it's been dredged and quite large ships use it with cargoes of timber and brandy. I remember the brandy boats because one of my sons worked on them for a time. I worked on my son to get me some free brandy. Quite in vain, of course, which showed how well I must have brought my sons up if it showed nothing else.

Often my mother and her 'brothers' would be given a loaf and some cheese and sent out for the day to get them from under their mother's skirts. Their only instruction was to be back when it got dark. It's strange how parents had no fear for their children's safety. They didn't need to. There was no fast road traffic and nobody it seemed ever molested children. Instinctively everyone mistrusted strangers and children would run from them if they saw them, but people rarely moved around except for a purpose, so a strange face was a rarity. Nobody in a village community would dare to assault anyone sexually. They would be bound to be found out and it would be like solitary confinement —no work—no social life. People today say that punishment is no deterrent to crime. In those days it most certainly was and in most of my working life too. It was the consequences that kept me on the straight and narrow.

Every village had a village idiot or idiots, but although they were teased it was done with kindliness and if ever they were ill or needed help there were always those who would go to their aid.

Most cottage gardens were given over entirely to vegetables and mum's was no exception. All ground that you owned or rented was a means of getting food either through pigs, poultry or vegetables. Anybody that grew flowers was wasteful or an eccentric. But mum said there was a great variety of wild flowers around in the fields and lanes. This was her flower garden. I remember when she used to take us out on walks around Hove she'd be able to give a name to any flower we pointed out to her —not the Latin names which I believe they all have—the pretty names the country people used to give them, like ragged robin. Nowadays when people take their children for a walk in Hove they reel off the names of cars that are parked in the kerb or flying by along the roads. That's progress for you.

As well as the flowers there were fruits in their season: blackberries, sloes, crab-apples, watercress, mushrooms and nuts; as well, of course, as the windfalls from the trees in the farm orchards; and as mum says, if there wasn't any wind about at the time one of her brothers would be ready to climb the tree and shake the fruit into their waiting hands.

One of the tastes I miss today is of real mushrooms. Generally cultivation makes things taste better. All it's done to mushrooms is to make them look like buttons, all more or less of a size and taste like cork.

Then mum says there was often something going on in the streets. There'd be the patter of the 'street persuaders', the travelling salesmen who wandered from village to village selling or bartering their wares. A lot of this bartering went on; the goods they got in exchange for what they were selling serving as wares for the next village. There were the street 'doctors' with medicines that could cure a hundred ailments. 'Under the counter cures' for unwanted pregnancies. As mum says it wasn't what they sold, it was the way that they sold them that fascinated her. It was another of her party tricks when we were children for her to rattle out this salesman spiel. She'd go on for about five minutes and keep the whole family in stitches. She had, and still has, a marvellous memory. Too good for comfort sometimes.

Once a month as regular as clockwork an organ grinder would appear, with a bear on a collar and chain. There the organ grinder would stand, bear chain in one hand and winding away at the organ with the other. Then he'd give a hard tug on the chain and the reluctant bear would start dancing. Mum says she felt sorry for it, it had such a mournful face. Still all the bears I have seen have mournful faces. The only time they look amused is when they're snarling. I reckon as with some people, bears' appearances can be deceptive. In any case a great many of us have to dance to somebody else's tune and we don't look miserable doing it—not all the time at any rate.

In the summer there would be the acrobats, the rope walkers and the trapeze artists. They used the streets as their circus ring, putting up their ropes and swings across the street. It must have been a hazardous way to earn a few pence because they used no nets in case they fell; and although it was a great treat for the village nobody could afford to contribute much, and of course the children gave nothing. Although mum says she never saw the performers come to any harm there used to be a lot of bruises and sprains among the kids of the village for weeks after they had left, with them trying to emulate the performers on tree boughs and along the tops of walls.

Another more frequent source of amusement was the town crier with his three-cornered hat and hand bell. He'd walk the streets crying, 'Notice! Notice!' and the children following behind would shout, 'Notice! Notice! Red-hot Poultice!' He was a man of great dignity, mum says, 'He never chased us or reported us to our parents, he just carried on as if we were not there.' She compared him to the Pied Piper of Hamelin—a poem that was read in every school at that time. I reckon that he must often have wished he was, so that he could have led the kids into some hillside and carried on his job without interference.

So, as mum says, though things were pretty cruel at home for her, her world outside was a compensation so that like many old people she can at times say that parts of her childhood were the happiest days of her life. She is able to reject the wretchedness from her memory when she wants to.

I must also say that though when I was younger and she told us the harrowing stories of the way she was treated I was full of sympathy, I have since wondered as to how much she herself goaded people into treating her badly. All right, when she was hit she couldn't hit back, but I can imagine the kind of dumb insolence with which she would suffer punishment. How her face would fall into a sullen kind of waxwork expression which said: 'Well, you've hit me and you've knocked me around and where's it got you? I won't let you see how you hurt me, I won't howl, I won't cry.' It's this sort of passive defiance that drives people on to more violent action till they can see that they've broken you at last. I feel sure that is what she was like then, because at times that is the kind of nature she has now. Not, I hasten to add, that we use violence on her.

Nowadays I think most children look forward to Sundays. For

mum and her brothers it was a dour sort of day. They had to dress in their best clothes. This in itself was restricting because they were not allowed outside in them until they went to church in case they should romp about and get dirt on their shoes. 'Church,' mum says, 'I found a great trial, a great trial. The service was far too long and in a language which even though we were Church of England I didn't recognise or understand. In his sermons, bits of which I did understand, and more's the pity, the preacher would drone on about salvation. For him the whole idea (for us poor things anyway) was to get through life as quickly as possible and with as few sins as possible (and I hadn't much idea about sinning or what it really meant) so that we could die and get to the place called paradise. Since nobody, no matter how badly they are being treated, wants to die when they are kids, and since my idea of paradise was getting away from home as soon as possible (that was the salvation I was seeking), I thought at that time that religion was a load of old codswallop.

'After church came Sunday dinner. This was a meal to look forward to because it was often the only meat we children got during the week. When it was over though I used to have to do the washing up, swathed in an apron that was much too big for me to make sure I didn't sully my Sunday best. By the time I'd finished it was time for Sunday School and off my brothers and I would troop to church once again. Sunday School. Now there's a stupid waste of time, or it was in those days. There were all the children gathered together with ages ranging from three to thirteen—there were even some babes in arms carried there by their brothers and sisters and they were no respecters of the House of God. Then once again we were treated to all the high falutin' talk way above our heads about souls, saints and sinners; and about heaven and how to get there. I remember thinking, Supposing someone had come into the church and taken me by the hand and said: "Come on, I'm going to take you up to heaven. It's a lovely place where you can play with toys all day long and have lovely food, lots of manna and honey, and you can sound your brass and tinkle your cymbals." I'd have said, "Not likely, you're not. It may not be much of a life down here yet but

I'm prepared to give it time, I'm not swopping it for what you and old starch collar there have to offer." Mind you,' mum went on to say, 'every cloud has a silver lining, and for Sunday School it was the Sunday School Treat. Once a year in the summer the farmers used to draw up their drays outside the church. We kids would all pile in and we'd be driven to a meadow where there were organised sports and games. I was a good runner and as there were money prizes I'd win sixpence or eightpence during the afternoon and that was a lot of money at that time. Not that it did me any good, my mother took it off me when I got home to keep it for me for a rainy day. I never saw it again. Not that I minded. I felt I proved something to myself and to the world by winning. Mind you,' she said, 'this didn't compensate for the dismal boredom of fifty-two Sundays a year.'

Once again mum was inconsistent because she packed her children off to Sunday School in just the same way. We didn't have to go to morning service, but in the afternoon we suffered the same agonies of boredom and incomprehension that she had. I tackled her about this a few years ago and she felt she was justified: 'There we were a family of eight, dad and me and you six kids, living in three rooms. Your dad and me had very little time ever to ourselves. He'd finish work Saturday dinner-time, do some odd jobs around the house in the afternoon, then take me to the pub in the evening. Sunday, he spent on the allotment and Sunday afternoon once we'd got you kids out of the way was an ideal time for love-making. We could go to bed and do it in freedom and comfort.' Mum chuckled a bit as she related this. 'I've never told that to a living soul before. Not even to my closest friend. In my day it wasn't considered respectable to make love in the daylight.' 'No more it wasn't in mine,' I said. It was funny talking to my mother about sex. It was the first time in my life she'd ever discussed it with me. We never had any of those cosy little chats that parents have with their children today. I can't say that I've missed them.

Mum's Sunday devotions at Shoreham didn't finish with Sunday School. 'It was the era of the family Bible,' she said. 'After tea father would go to the dresser where the Bible was kept. He had sort of book markers in the pages he most enjoyed reading. He'd find his place, sit at the head of the table, stare around us and when he thought we were looking sufficiently devout he'd begin. He always read from the Old Testament and seemed to choose the bits where God or some king or leader of the time was taking it out on the children. Whether he felt he was sort of justifying his and mother's attitude towards me, I don't know. I know it gave me no love of God or of my parents. I remember at quite an early age deciding never to seek help from Him above. And I haven't.' I don't think mum ever has. I can't imagine she could. If anything went wrong in her life or ours she wouldn't go down on her knees, she'd go into action to put it right—and she generally did.

So except for Sunday dinner the Sabbath was a dead loss for working-class children, a day of gloom and mumbo-jumbo. I asked mum whether she thought the older people enjoyed it. 'Well, it was a day of rest in a way for the men and apart from the cooking for the women too. Most everybody went to church either in the morning or evening. It was habit, routine. For some it was a necessity because if they hadn't been seen there regularly by the people they worked for they'd have been sacked. For others it was a kind of insurance policy. They hoped that by regular attendance they would secure an easier life in the here-after. That's what they were told by the vicars, who were the sort of labour relations officers of the time. They persuaded people to put up with the treatment they were given by their bosses by promising them a place in heaven when they died. And people believed it. Some still do.'

I think that although mum is generalising there's a lot in what she says. There are a number of people who think that those who get money the easy way by backing horses or winning on the pools are ruined by it. If that's the case, why aren't all the people who make money on stocks and shares or take-over bids a lot of wrecks? I remember in one place where I was working as a kitchen-maid there was something I did wrong and I had to go to the drawing-room to be told off by the mistress of the house. It was during the Season and she'd been out to a lot of events and parties. 'Langley,' she said, 'you're an idle, selfish and inconsiderate girl. Here am I exhausted with all these late nights and I have to spend my days checking and correcting your work.' I remember thinking, 'You're pretty exhausted having a good time on ten thousand, why should I wear myself out on eighteen pounds a year?' I suppose one of those old parsons would have given me the answer.

One other thing mum remembers about Sunday was that it was the day they got a newspaper—*Lloyd's Sunday News* it was. Today that wouldn't mean anything to a little girl who, even if she could read, wouldn't be interested in what was in the papers, but, because her mother couldn't read, her father used to read bits out loud. Generally they were the spicy murder stories and an early memory of mum's was the Jack the Ripper scare. His killings were done with a desire to mutilate the victims sexually and by someone with a considerable knowledge of the human body. There were five such killings that were put down to Jack the Ripper in 1888, but several others were attributed to him by the sensational press in later years. Naturally mum used to listen avidly as her dad read out the details, but she used to suffer for it. Now mum had a great fear of the dark because a frequent punishment was for her to have to stand in the coal shed or in the cupboard under the stairs, so she became terrified of even going out in the dark—and if she did she was continually frightened by the image of Jack the Ripper. Even hearing the newsboys shouting: 'Another 'orrible murder—Jack the Ripper's at it again!' was enough to send her running for home. When I asked her why and explained that after all she must have known that Jack the Ripper was in London, she was quite unselfish about her fears—'I was afraid he had heard that that newsboy was spreading it around about him and would come down and murder him.'

Then there was another more legendary figure that used to haunt mum's fantasies: 'Spring-Heeled Jack'. She talked about him as though he was a contemporary of Jack the Ripper. He wasn't; he was the Marquis of Waterford and was practising his tricks of jumping out and frightening people long before her time, at the beginning of the nineteenth century.

Other people copied him down the years and the title was given to them. The Spring-Heeled Jack that so terrified my mother was a London thief that the police couldn't catch because of his agility in jumping over walls and hedges. He was an extension for my mother's fantasies, because whenever she was walking by a high wall or fence she couldn't feel safe from attack. I suppose most of us suffer from similar fears today, though I doubt if they are inspired by our parents' attitude towards us. But mum, even at the time when I would have thought her life wasn't worth living, was quite philosophical about it. 'There was one thing used to comfort me,' she said; 'I knew life couldn't get much worse so I could look forward to it getting better.' A little of her philosophy must have rubbed off on to me because when I first went into service there would be complaints about my work both from madam upstairs and the cook below, and one of the footmen would try and take advantage of my low morale by getting me in a dark corner. Although I objected to it and managed to reject him, it was good to know somebody fancied you.

Another annual event in Shoreham that my mother had to look forward to was the Regatta. She wasn't so much interested in the races, but the day was more of a carnival. There were swings and roundabouts and sideshows. Mum particularly remembers seeing men on stilts for the first time with long trousers down to their feet. She thought they were some new race which had descended on the earth, and it was a long time before she could be convinced that they were balancing on wooden struts. Then there were the Hokey-Pokey ice-cream sellers. Mum was given a water ice, the cheapest kind. It was served in a shallow glass dish and you licked it out of this. No spoons were provided. Then you handed it back and another ice-cream was served in it for the next person. There was no washing it up. Not very hygienic, but, as mum says, in those days people swallowed so many germs they either died of them or were inoculated against diseases.

Then there were the crab sellers, with their live crabs in baskets, selling at fourpence each. Mum tells of how she and other kids used to stand behind them and wait till they were occupied making a sale. Then they'd tip the basket and let out a few crabs which went scuttling around taking advantage of their freedom. The crab man couldn't chase the kids because he was too busy rescuing his wares but he used to swear at them 'something horrible'. Another innocent childish amusement she used to indulge in was to buy a farthing's worth of scorched peas and shoot them out of her mouth on to the backs of the people watching the Regatta. It's funny the habits parents will confess to as they get older.

There must at some time have been an attempt at Shoreham to cash in on the popularity of Brighton and Hove because in 1838 Shoreham's noted Swiss Gardens were opened. There they had bowls, archery, rowing on a lake, caves and grottoes, refreshment rooms and a theatre. It turned out to be somebody's Folly because by mum's day it had fallen on very hard times. There were a few things going on there, but of course you had to pay to go in, which mum was never able to.

Guy Fawkes night even now is an event in every town and village in Sussex. Then it was looked forward to, and prepared for, months ahead. A great bonfire was built and lit on the Ham, a piece of common ground, people put on fancy dress and daubed their faces with rouge or burnt cork and a tar barrel was lit and rolled down the street on to the Ham. Shops used to put up their shutters and reinforce them with planks, but mum remembers how one shopkeeper who was unpopular had his torn down and used as fuel for the bonfire.

On Brighton race days and particularly during the Sussex fortnight when horse racing was taking place somewhere in the county, there would be a lot of traffic passing through Shoreham. The children used to run along the roadside turning cartwheels, leapfrogging and somersaulting in the hope that a coin or two would be flung to them from the passing carriages and there was always a penny or two to be earned by holding the horses outside the village inn.

Brighton market days were an excuse for another childish amusement. The market carts used to leave Shoreham loaded early in the morning and return empty in the late afternoon. The goods were packed in large wicker baskets, some of which hung on hooks from the back of the carts so low that they almost reached the ground. The horses were tired after the double trip and as they ambled back it was easy for children to clamber into the baskets and get the fun of a ride. The driver knew when he'd got illegal passengers because the cart got weighed down but he was often as tired as his horses and would suffer them. This, of course, didn't suit the kids; it wasn't exciting enough, so they'd bounce up and down or tease the driver. Then up would go the cry 'Whip behind!' and the driver would flail his whip and the children would try to escape it by ducking into the baskets. If things got too out of hand the driver would stop his cart and try to catch the culprits. Since getting out of the baskets was more difficult than getting in he'd often succeed and reward the captive with a box across the ears. This was accepted as part of the game by the victim. If he'd gone home and complained to his parents about it he would have ended up with another good hiding.

Chapter Two

It was school that was the centre of life for mum. She went in 1884 when she was four years old. The building is still there though it is no longer used as a school. They built to last in those days. About fifty children attended and there were two classes. Although education was compulsory, it wasn't free. It was three-pence a week for the first child, tuppence for the second and a penny each for any subsequent children. Naturally there was a lot of absenteeism because parents couldn't afford the money. Technically if they really couldn't pay they could get exemption and the child or children would be given a form to take to school. But this was degrading to both the parents and the children and in those days you kept yourself to yourself, you didn't want anybody knowing your business and husbands never let their wives know what they were earning. Again a lot of parents who were illiterate themselves couldn't see the point of this new fangled so-called education. They'd got on all right without it, so why shouldn't their children. I can understand this point of view. My husband Albert took a lot of persuading that it was right for our boys to go to grammar school and we suffered by sending them there. Not just financially. Since we couldn't afford to buy the right kit for games they were largely excluded from playing them. Then their class would be asked who was entitled to free meals and books and theirs would be the only three hands to go up. Then during the last war when I hadn't the money to get new shoes I got a voucher from the Town Hall. This only entitled them to a special sort of boots and none of the other boys wore boots. I know that to some extent my boys were made to feel socially inferior and psychologically this takes a lot of getting over in later life.

It is interesting that at that time in Shoreham there were un-official school dinners. At dinner-time the children would assemble in St Mary's Church Hall and for a halfpenny they would get a bowl of soup—good soup, mum says, with bits of meat in—and a slice of bread and jam. Mum much preferred this to dinner at home because in the church hall she could laugh and talk as she had it, whereas at home she was not allowed to speak and there was no gaiety or friendliness.

Although mum didn't think so at the time conditions at the school were rather primitive. There was one cold tap in the school yard under which children used to put their mouths if they wanted a drink and which got frozen up in the winter so they had to do without. There were no washing places and since there was no sanitation for lavatories they had six buckets in a row of cubicles which were used by both girls and boys, so going to the loo was quite a social occasion.

A number of children who attended the school were 'the workhouse brats' as they were called by their class mates. There were many more in the winter when work was scarce. Then whole families went into the workhouse to try to keep alive until the summer. It was an inhuman system. The husbands were separated from their wives, and the children from both; each had their own dormitories and their own eating places. The idea seemed to be to make the workhouse such a horrifying place that people would do their utmost to keep out of it. In the summer mum remembers that once a month the inmates who were mostly old people were allowed to go around the town knocking at the doors to ask for a little money or a gift. Nearly everyone no matter how poor they were themselves gave something.

At school the workhouse children were easily distinguished from the others because they all had the same uniform—the girls grey cotton dresses in the summer and navy wool ones in the winter. The boys wore a sort of rough serge winter and summer.

They kept completely apart from the other children and of course no ordinary child was allowed to mix with a workhouse brat after school; nor indeed was the opportunity given.

The house where mum lived backed on to the workhouse, which was surrounded by a high wall like a prison. She remembers hearing the children playing and laughing behind the wall and wishing she was one of them. They may have been treated like lepers but at least they seemed happy. Not that she dared voice this opinion even to her school friends. You had to keep in with the herd to make life endurable and children could be very, very cruel. Being in a minority at any time in mum's early life could make things pretty appalling, she says. I must say nowadays she makes up for lost opportunities!

Apart from the fact that it got her away from home mum liked school. She enjoyed learning and she was good at it. This gave her some importance which helped to make life more bearable. But she led a sort of Jekyll-and-Hyde existence because the moment she went back home she had to lose any feelings of self-esteem and become humble, unopinionated and servile.

Mum got on well with all her teachers. The main subjects, of course, were the three Rs, reading, writing and arithmetic. There were no organised games or physical training though they did do what was called drill; and they had nature study which again mum enjoyed because it made her more aware of the country around her. Although the cane was used fairly regularly she talks of the teachers as being devoted to their work. They tried hard to get results even from the dullest children. She thinks this was because compulsory education hadn't been long introduced and the teachers looked on their jobs as a challenge. It was difficult for parents and the older children to see the purpose behind it, after all there were only the same old jobs waiting for them afterwards. For mum there was no 'brave new world' around the corner.

Needlework was the one subject mum disliked, probably, she thinks, because she had to do so much of it at home in the evenings, also they had to make uninspiring things like chemises and bloomers from hard stiff calico. The girls who made the best garments were allowed to go round the town selling them and there was never any lack of buyers because they cost very little more than the materials. They were also taught to do crochet work, but knitting was unknown at that time.

Naturally mum made a number of friends with other girls but nobody really close because friendships were never able to ripen out of school. Once or twice she would go to other girls' homes for tea, but since she couldn't return their hospitality their invitations stopped and as she wasn't allowed out in the evenings she couldn't enjoy that part of her friends' lives.

The few visits she made to other people's houses enabled mum to contrast them with the conditions she lived in. This was particularly true in her father's brother's home. He and his wife had two children, Mary Jane and John Thomas, and the relationships between them and their parents really astonished mum. She found it hard to believe that children and their parents could laugh, joke and have fun together, and that a family could get such a lot of pleasure out of each other's company. Her Uncle Bob would tease her and romp about with her, tossing her into the air and then running around with her on his shoulders, but eventually her mother put an end to that. 'Stop it, Bob!' she yelled out. 'Stop messing around with that child. Can't you see she's spoilt enough already.' That was that. Their relationship was never the same afterwards.

Mum sees education as the start of the split in the family life of this country. Children's brains were being exercised and developed for the first time on a large scale; a quite considerable degree of authority was being transferred from the parents to the teachers. Children's reasoning powers became greater than those of their parents and the expression, 'Teacher says that...' came into many of the arguments between them. No longer was there the blind sense of love, acceptance and obedience. In relating it to herself mum once again used religion. 'Until I was about eleven,' she says, 'I believed in the story of Adam and Eve and the Garden of Eden. Then I began thinking about it and one day went to my teacher and talked to her. She told me it was a sort of legend made up to impress simple people and to look on it as that. I didn't tell them at home of course. After that I began questioning a lot of other things.'

The main, indeed the only, amusement for the grown-ups, as mum still calls them, was the pub, and a village pub in those days was very different from the Swedish pine, velvet-curtained, phony brass-fitted, deep-carpeted places you get today. It was real 'spit and sawdust'. Scrubbed board floors and cuspidors which the men would shoot into with incredible accuracy. The value for money that you looked for was in the drink not in the surroundings, and you found it. According to mum half a pint of beer could put hairs on a man's chest. Why putting hairs on his chest should be a man's ambition I don't know, neither when I taxed her with it did mum. I thought men were trying to get away from their forefathers the apes. I also asked mum how she knew the drink was so good and strong. 'I sampled it, didn't I?' she replied. 'How?' I asked. 'Well, when mother was breast feeding my younger brothers I'd have to go to the pub and fetch her half a pint of porter. It helped her with the milk.' 'Did it put hairs on her chest?' I couldn't resist it. She ignored that remark. 'It cost a penny a half pint and was handed to me in a sort of small tin bucket with a lid on top, and always on the way home I'd have a sip of it. Beautiful stuff it was, did something for you, I got the taste for it young.' I reminded her how she used to send me round to the jug and bottle bar when I was a girl. 'I never dared sip it,' I said. 'You used to measure it out in a glass afterwards and if there'd been any short you'd have sent me back.' She ignored that remark too. Still, I also got the taste for it soon enough.

Of course in mum's day there were no restrictions on drinking hours. It was quite a frequent sight to see men queuing up for a drink at six in the morning. The pub was the club for the working man. It was the only relaxation and entertainment he got. There was precious little comfort in the home which was sparsely furnished, ill-lit and alive with kids. For mum's father it must have been a refuge.

Although she can recall her mother vividly, her picture of her father in indistinct. She thinks it's because he was out of the house for so much of the time. His work started at six in the morning and finished at six at night. He did generally have a half-day on Saturday but this was the exception rather than the rule with the working class. When he came home he would wash and shave, eat his evening meal which was called 'dad's tea' and then walk to the pub. It wasn't that he was a heavy drinker, he probably only had a pint or a pint and a half of beer each evening, but there he could talk to his fellows, play cards, skittles or dominoes, and feel important. In fact her father was important. As an engineering worker he was considered to be a skilled man, moreover he could read. Every evening when he went in the landlord would hand him the newspaper. He'd go through it and would then read out loud the bits which he thought would be of interest so that his listeners did really hang on his words. After he'd read a passage he would pass judgement on it, so her father's opinion and the news must often have got mixed up in the minds of his mates. Politically he was a liberal with leftish tendencies, at least that's how I interpret it when mum says he read the *Daily Chronicle* and criticised the bosses. He also had a quick temper and was for ever falling out with his fellow workers. As a result he had to change his jobs from time to time. Unlike the farm labourers mum's father was not afraid to speak his mind or perhaps, she thinks, he couldn't help it. Many men at that time had always to keep a close watch on their tongues. If it was reported back that they had criticised their employers or even voiced different political opinions they were likely to get the sack, and since their homes were tied to their jobs they would then have to leave those as well; and when they came to look for another job word would have been put around about them and there would be nothing left for them and their families but the workhouse. So the expression 'Freedom of Speech' had a hollow ring about it.

According to mum her father was a very patriotic man, always exhorting everyone to go down on their knees and thank God they were British. Compared with any foreigners we were little gods and the envy of the rest of the world. Mum therefore, under her circumstances, pitied these foreigners. Dad's patriotic fervour was given full rein on the day of Queen Victoria's Diamond Jubilee, mum says. 'It was a national holiday though we children had to go to school and march around the playground singing songs and waving flags and queuing up to be presented with a china mug each. Then we went back home. Mother was cooking a special meal, same as on Sundays, and dad had gone for a walk round the town ending with a visit to the pub. It came to dinner-time but dad didn't appear. As he was generally punctual mum sent one of the boys round to the pub to tell him it was ready. Neither dad nor my brother appeared. The dinner was spoiling and so was mother's temper. "Go and see where they've got to and don't hang about, come straight back," she barked at my younger brother. Time went by and still nobody returned. Mother's face was like thunder and I wished myself anywhere but where I was. I was waiting expecting to be the next to have to go and find them. Then dad appeared in the doorway. "Where do you think you've been?" mother screamed. Even I, young as I was, thought it an unnecessary question. "Getting drunk in the Queen's name," shouted dad, as though that put it right; then he staggered to the chair by the fireplace and passed out before mother could say another word. Give her her due, she was a good wife, she took his boots off and loosened his neckband before she turned on the boys, "And why didn't you come back like I told you?" "He wouldn't let us," they said, but it was no good, they both got the full force of her hand around their ears. "Get out and don't come back until tea time," she yelled. "You too," pointing at me. I walked obediently to follow my brothers. "And take that stupid expression off your face," and she caught me one around the head which sent me flying through the door. We wandered around trying to feel gay and patriotic. When we returned home it was like a morgue. There was dad looking grey and sheepish and mother with a set expression on her face. We ate the meal which was to have been our dinner, in silence, and trooped up to bed as soon as we could. I was only seven, yet Queen Victoria's jubilee will always stand out in my memory. It was the only time I ever saw dad drunk, and the only time I can remember him making a funny remark, even if it was an unconscious one.'

Mum says the closest she got to her father was when she was making or repairing his clothes. For work he wore white corduroy trousers, they may have started as a light grey but they soon washed white, and a white cotton jacket they called 'slops'. It's a sort of naval expression. He didn't wear underpants such as we know them today. Mum had to make him calico linings which she sewed into his trousers and which got washed with his trousers once a week. By working-class standards her father was a very clean man since men who wore trousers made of darker material only had them washed every three weeks or so. On Sundays he wore a black suit and since this was just sponged and ironed, the linings had to be taken out to be washed and then sewn in again; another dreary job for mum. Again mum had to make all his shirts. These were cut out from flannel material. They had a neckband but no collar. On weekdays he would wear a scarf around his neck for work and change this for a kerchief in the evening. For Sundays he had special dark red or blue spotted kerchiefs.

All water had to be fetched from a well at the end of the street, another job for the children. Mum says she doesn't remember having a bath. There wasn't a sink or a tin bath, only an iron copper. Every Saturday night though, her father would strip to the waist, sit on a chair and her mother would wash him, even his face and his ears. She didn't do the same for her children; godliness and cleanliness didn't go hand in hand for them.

Newspapers were used to the full in those days. They served as wrappings in shops, as handkerchiefs, as spills to light pipes and as lavatory paper.

So mum's life until she was thirteen was set against this rural unchanging background. Her home was unloving, austere and punctuated with mental and physical cruelty. Her school she enjoyed but her education was, as it were, an end in itself. It couldn't lead her anywhere. She would leave school knowing how to read, write and with the elementary knowledge of arithmetic she'd need for the day-to-day buying and selling. It couldn't help her to shape her destiny—the pattern of her life had been decided on the day she was born. It was only the detail that the future could fill in. At the age of thirteen she could only look back with thanks that she had survived and look forward confident that what was to come couldn't be as bad as what had been.

Chapter Three

It was just after her thirteenth birthday that mum's father came back home from work and said, 'I'm done with Holloways.' That meant that he was finished with the electrical firm for whom he worked. They had probably in fact finished with him because although, as mum says, he was a skilled and hard worker he had an evil temper and he was hated by those who worked with him. He had lost jobs before for that reason. This mum had learnt from other people's children at school. 'What are you going to do?' her mother asked. 'I'm finished with Holloways and I'm finished with bloody Shoreham,' was the reply which ended the conversation for that evening.

The next day mum's father was up early as usual and left the house. He came back later that evening and announced that he'd got a job at the Corporation Water Works in Hove, he was starting the following Monday, he'd fixed himself some lodgings, he'd give the job a month and that if it worked out all right they'd up sticks and move there. Again that was all the conversation for that night. Nobody was asked whether they had any objections to the move. A pronouncement had been made and would be acted upon. 'But surely your mother would have discussed it with him later,' I said. Mum didn't think so. 'Just as children knew their place, and behaved accordingly, women knew theirs. The expression "A woman's place is in the home" meant more than it said. It meant that a woman ruled over the home, its furnishings, its cleaning, the cooking, the bringing up of the children, the making of clothes. These were the things on which the woman made the decisions which were seldom questioned, but the major issues were decided by the man. It wasn't a bad thing either,' confided mum. 'Anyway it worked and so did marriages.' 'But all this wasn't true of the upper classes', I said. 'Of course not', mum replied. 'But people today don't understand what class distinction really was. In country places there were two classes and most people were born into the working class. I suppose the odds were about a thousand to one. Both classes had their own set of rules. The working class never did anything the upper classes did. They didn't go to the same places, didn't eat the same food, didn't wear the same kind of clothes. You could tell at a glance to which class anybody belonged and woe betide any working-class person who tried to get above his station. He was despised by both classes. This business of knowing your place was the accepted way of life of the time. There were of course the reformers that you read about in your history books, but for every reformer there were thousands of conformers who were contented with their lot.'

So mum's father, with hardly more than a day out of work, started his new job in Hove. I was a bit astonished that he was able to get work so quickly and without a reference because it was obvious he hadn't had a chance to get one. 'It was him being a skilled man,' mum said. 'In those days engineers were scarce. All right they hadn't got "O" levels or "A" levels or a string of letters after their names. They learnt their job by doing it and employers would be able to size a man up by the previous work he'd done and he'd also take him on because he liked the look of him. Today of course it's different. You've got to show on paper that you've got the qualifications and no longer does a prospective employer "like the look of you". I suppose this is because the business of employing people has got so large that it has become mechanised. In those days firms would employ, say, ten to fifty people so that the boss knew them all individually and felt he had to get the best out of them. Socially the boss and his workers would be miles apart but during the day they were drawn together. They were mates on Christian name terms and often real friends.

That's why this "liking the look of you" was so important.'

It seems a bit strange today that mum's father had to go into digs when Shoreham was only ten miles away, but commuting was out of the question; there just wasn't the transport. Anyway he must have liked his job and his face must have fitted there because at the end of a month he decided that the family would move.

This was a momentous decision as far as mum was concerned. Her feelings were mixed. She hated the idea of leaving the places she had known all her life, the fields, the school, the shops and her friends. These were her security. On the other hand there was the excitement of going somewhere new, of living in a town, of a new home and the beginning a new phase in her life because now she wouldn't be going back to school, she would start work and eventually would be able to get away from her parents.

I wondered whether there was not another consideration which mum hadn't spoken of, boy friends. After all at thirteen I thought she might have formed some sort of association with boys. She hadn't. 'Children of thirteen in my day were still children,' she said. 'There was never any question of us using lipstick, rouge or powder or dressing up. We looked like children and emotionally and perhaps even mentally we were the same as a nine-year-old today. Boys to me then were just the opposite sex, another aspect of humanity—or of inhumanity.'

'Didn't it strike you that you would be moving closer to your real mother and that you'd be able to see more of her?' I said. 'I was hoping you wouldn't say that,' said mum. 'You hadn't seemed to notice that I hadn't mentioned her except once or twice at the beginning of my life. It makes me feel wretched and unhappy even today to think about it. You see as I told you those visits by that lady meant so much to me. I remember the last time she came to see me. She'd put me to bed and told me a story, then she went downstairs. I heard voices raised. It was she and my pretended mother quarrelling. I got out of bed, opened the door and listened. The gist of it was that my "mother" was telling her that she couldn't come to see me again. "She'll start asking questions about you, then the fat will be in the fire." She went on to say that she must make up her mind whether to take me with her or stop seeing me altogether. I remember my heart doing an extra bump at that. I wanted so much for her to say she would. She didn't though. I heard her leave the house. I waited for the following month to come round without saying anything. She didn't come and I realised then that she never would again. It was the last I saw of her. I didn't speak to anyone about it. It was, and has been, my secret. A horrid one to have.'

This was another thing that my mother had to live with as a child. She didn't know the nice lady was her mother, but she knew the happiness and love she brought with her. Now she had been outlawed—and by her 'mother'.

Just before she left Shoreham her mother received a visit which had she acted upon it differently might have changed the course of mum's life. One of the governors of the school mum went to came to ask if she could be allowed to return to school as a pupil teacher. She would be found lodgings and would go to Hove every weekend. They don't have these pupil teachers today. To be one meant that you were considered bright enough to take the classes for the younger children—the infants. As you got older and more experienced you could be elevated to being an uncertificated teacher. That was one who hadn't been to a training college but had learnt by doing. It wasn't as well paid as a real teacher's job, but it was a deal better than going into any other kind of employment that was likely to be open to mum.

When she heard about it mum's imagination took over. She visualised herself returning to school in triumph. Meeting her friends not as just another girl in their class but in a position of authority. For the first time in her life she would be giving orders and telling people what to do, even if they were only four or five years old.

She needn't have bothered with these flights of fancy. Predictably her mother refused to consider the idea even though the family could have afforded to do without the little mum was likely to bring in by going out to work. It was the old story. Mum was illegitimate and must suffer because of it.

People have said to me how strange it was that the slur of

illegitimacy was so strong when by examining church registers of the time it was apparent that christenings came too hot on the heels of marriages for respectability; particularly in country villages most girls didn't get married unless they were pregnant. But it was the fact that they did marry the father that made it all right. The great fear was getting pregnant and not knowing or not being sure who the father was or his refusing to marry you. It was probably this fear which made people in some areas countenance and even encourage 'bundling'—where a prospective suitor used to climb in through his girl friend's window and get into bed with her. According to the rules they played around but didn't go the whole hog. I reckon it's like football, if the truth were known a lot of names would have been taken!

The day of the move was quite an event not only for mum's family but for the whole of Shoreham. Mostly people moved around in the town with the heavy possessions being shifted by hand cart with the man pushing and cursing and the rest of the family following behind laden with the lighter articles, looking like people fleeing from the pestilence or refugees escaping from a war. This one though was done with a removal van and horses and they were going into a brand new house. Of course they weren't buying the house, it was rented. All houses built for the working class were to rent, nobody dreamed of buying one, there wasn't the money nor were there the facilities. In any case often houses went with the job. Not free but they were owned and let by the boss. This gave him an additional hold on his workers. If they didn't turn up he could soon send round to find out why and always there was the threat that if you got the sack you also lost your home. This house by any standards of the time was a good one. It had six rooms and the rent was eight shillings a week. There was no bathroom nor a hot water system and the lavatory was outside, but that was the rule in those days. Rates of course were in with the rent but this didn't cause the landlord much hardship as the rates were low, very little being provided as service in those days. It may seem astonishing that mum knew what the rent was in view of the secrecy about family matters at the time, but you didn't pay rent; it was taken from you by the rent collector who called once a week and, since rent collectors weren't very popular people, the children were sent to the door to give them the money. Sometimes they'd go there to stave the rent collector off when he couldn't be paid. Rent was one of the uncertain factors in life at that time. Most prices remained more or less stable but often the rent would be put up. This could upset any household where the money was budgeted for to the nearest halfpenny. It riled the tenants and made 'landlord' a dirty word. Eviction of course was much easier and it was a commonplace to see a family sitting on the pavement surrounded by their furniture and possessions and with no place to go.

Old opinions as well as old customs die hard, which I think accounts for the almost punitive legislation against landlords today.

Another thing mum knew which surprises me was that her mother got thirty shillings a week housekeeping money. Every Friday night her father would give her two gold coins, a sovereign and a half a sovereign. 'Money looked and felt like money in those days,' she says.

For the first fortnight in Hove mum was kept busy with household jobs, sewing curtains and generally getting the place in order. Then her mother announced that she must get a job. The newspaper was studied and one was found for her. It was as maid of all work to a boarding-house, a daily job which started at seven in the morning and ended at five in the evening. For this she got one and sixpence a week and her breakfast and dinner. It must have been a dreadful baptism of fire for her. I've only once worked in a boarding-house. It was called a guest house in my day but by any name these places smell the same, of stale boiled cabbage and cod. The first thing she had to do when she got there was to fill about a dozen white enamel sort of kettles with hot water, take them up, deposit them outside the bedrooms, knock on the door and shout out the time. This was no mean task as the water had to be poured from an enormous heavy copper kettle which was boiling on the kitchen range; there was no running hot water; there was one tap over the kitchen sink and that ran cold. Since the house was on four floors there was a lot of rushing up and down stairs and even when she'd finished and was helping lay and prepare the breakfast she'd continually be interrupted and told to give so and so another call as he was a heavy sleeper. If anyone did oversleep it was she who got the blame. 'That bloody little skivvy of yours didn't call me,' they'd say. Serving breakfast was an ordeal in itself. 'People's tempers were always at their worst first thing in the morning,' mum says. I suppose that's true of today too. 'They used to use the foulest language and they'd compare what they were given to eat to the most disgusting things. Mind you, if they'd seen where and the way it was cooked and handled I don't think they'd have eaten at all. Fortunately I had to do my own afterwards.' After breakfast she washed up and the woman of the house did the drying. 'That was the worst of this job,' mum says. 'Whatever work I was doing she was with me and always keeping on at me. "Get on with it, you lazy little sod," was her constant cry. It's funny though, because although it shook me at first, she called it me so often that it almost became a term of endearment.' It's true that, isn't it? Like with men who use foul language every second word it ceases to have any force or meaning. After breakfast was washed up she and the woman used to start on the rooms, making the beds, cleaning and dusting around. 'They didn't get much done to them,' mum says. 'There wasn't time. Anyway there wasn't much furniture, just an iron bed and a wash stand; for the regulars a chest of drawers and there weren't many of them, and in one of the corners a sort of wooden bracket with a curtain behind which they could hang their clothes. There was lino on the floor but no rugs.' After the bedrooms were done mum was left on her own doing down the stairs, while the woman prepared the dinner. The stairs weren't a great problem since they were lino and wooden slats but as I've said there were a lot of them and even at mum's tender age they were hard on the knees. Dinner wasn't like breakfast. Most of the lodgers didn't come back for it. After dinner wasn't so good though, because despite the fact that mum was on her own doing the dining-room, which also served as a sitting-room, and the outside steps, the woman of the house used to go out and on to the gin.

She'd come back a couple of hours later and revile mother 'something terrible'. Then the woman would go off, have a good cry and start preparing the teas which were a kind of hot supper. She served these herself though mum says she often left the washing up for her to do first thing the next morning.

In retrospect mum knows she was treated as a slavey but at the time she didn't see it that way. When she was abused by the woman or the lodgers it was impersonal abuse; something she could forget after it was given; but the abuse she got at home was personal. Her mother and her father would pick on her sensitive spots. They would pour salt on the tenderest of her wounds. So to her the job was in a way a relief. 'I had my thoughts,' she said, 'and in them I could imagine my mother before me starving, crying for me to throw her a crust of bread and I would turn away saying: "You showed me no kindness when I needed it, I'm not showing you any now." Or else I would see myself as being rich, a sort of ministering angel heaping coals of fire upon mother's head by bringing her gifts of money, delicacies and luxuries.' Servants had to live in a dream world in those days which accounted for the lurid magazines that were printed for them, things like *My Lady's Novelette* and *Red Letter*.

It was a soulless job, one in which there could be no relationships. There wasn't the opportunity or the time. Life there contained little incident. The lodgers were generally rough, kindly people who occasionally gave mum a copper or two when they left. They were mostly the commercial travellers of the time.

One or two things stand out in mum's memory. The woman once, after she'd been out on the gin all afternoon, came back more drunk than usual, but instead of wading into mum she gave her a lecture on the evils of drink. 'You probably think,' she said, 'that I've been drinking all afternoon, and you're right. But let me be a lesson to you. Before I met my late husband, God rot his soul, I'd never touched a drop. It was him, the wretched sod, that made me what I am today. But he got his just rewards. He was a jealous and a violent man and one night thinking that I had given my honour to the man at the bar I was talking to, he took a swipe at him, toppled over and fell down dead. Serve the bleeder right. He left me this house and a taste for gin.' Then she burst into tears, wiped her nose on a tea towel, sat down and went to sleep.

The rooms of the house were graded according to what floor they were on. Those on the first floor were the best and most expensive. The first floor front was let to an actor, who seemed to be permanently out of work. Herbert Vines his name was. Mum rather liked him because he was a bit out of the ordinary, and was often kind to her. He gave her strict instructions though never to go into his room until she had knocked and been told to come in. One day she forgot, and there was this Mr Vines dressed as a woman, with powder and lipstick on his face. When mum reported what had happened the woman of the house said, 'It's all right, he's rehearsing for a new play in which he has to dress up like that.' Since that was the last mum heard of the play she wondered what it was all about. Whenever she saw him she got this female image and it put her off him for good.

The cheapest rooms in the house were on the third floor. They were sort of attics with sloping roofs and small windows, like the servants' rooms which she and I were both to know later. One of these was for a time occupied by a young married couple. Mum had the greatest difficulty in getting into the room because they were always in bed. They tried to explain this away by saying that the room was so small and the ceiling so low, that this was the only position in which they could be comfortable and talk to each other. The landlady was not convinced. 'They're living in sin,' she said. 'No man who was married would want to spend that amount of time in bed with his wife. They'll have to go,' she added. 'I've always kept a respectable house, I'm not putting up with that kind of hanky panky.'

As she looks back on it the whole scene reminds mum of one of those old films where there are a couple on the run. They get to this seedy-looking house, are shown to a room with the bed sagging in the middle, there's a wash-stand with a cracked basin and jug and nothing else. They look around in a sort of half despair and the landlady says, 'Well, if you don't want it you know what you can do about it,' and they settle for the misery of the place, as she had to.

How mum suffered that job for a year is beyond my comprehension when I consider her spirit now. It must have been a sort of limbo period for her, a kind of dropping out, a time when she could build up her resources and feel ready to make the final break with her family. She was fifteen when she eventually went into domestic service proper. Looking back on my own life at her age, I experimented with jobs after leaving school but if I felt I was being hard done by I'd pack them in and get the support of my family when I did, particularly my father. I remember when I wanted to go to the laundry to work mum was dead set against it. People who were employed there were like fishwives according to her; foul language and worse behaviour. She was right of course but I suppose that made me want to go there the more and I got my way by wooing dad's support.

Chapter Four

The next job that mum got was through a registry office. She was walking home one day particularly browned off with the treatment she was getting at the boarding-house and at home when she noticed the place and decided to see what they had to offer.

Today when people talk about registry offices they mean places where people get married. In mum's day, and indeed in my early days, if you went to a registry office you were looking for domestic employment. There were many such places and even the smallest town would have one. Perhaps the most favoured was Mrs Hunt's in London. She catered only for the gentry or the very rich. Every day there would be a line of carriages drawn up outside Mrs Hunt's, later of course chauffeur-driven limousines. At one time she used to take commission both from the employers and the servants but there was some trouble about this and in my day only the employers had to pay. The quality of Mrs Hunt's wares was a constant topic of conversation in any drawing-room at that time.

There was a kind of apartheid in all registry offices: a room for the prospective employers which was comfortably and sometimes tastefully furnished and another with bare boards and hard benches for prospective domestics. There were cubicles for interviews. Mum says it was rather like visiting day at the jail. The interview in the registry office was only a sort of preliminary canter to see if your face suited. If it did there was a second interview when references were taken up and terms of employment agreed on.

Another way of getting work at that time was through the vicar. He was the sort of go-between of the upper and lower classes. He would know something of a person's upbringing and if you were the daughter of God-fearing people it was supposed to mean that you would work damned hard, unquestioningly, and that your morals would be all right. Employers attached great store to your morals. I must say this business of coming from God-fearing people I have found to be no criterion, because the sons and daughters of the clergy I have worked for were never any better than they should have been and some a great deal worse.

On mum's first visit to the registry office she just went to see what sort of jobs were going. There was one as a between-maid for which she was considered as a suitable applicant. I should think so too. A between-maid's lot was the most unhappy one in any household. You had to serve two masters, the cook and the housemaid. You were at the beck and call of either and if you were working for one the other would be screaming out for you to work for her. You were buffeted from pillar to post from morning to night. You could please neither and you were the centre of hostilities between the two parties. Give mum her due, when I was going into service she wouldn't consider me working as a between-maid and for this I had cause to be thankful.

Mum applied for and got this job. She gave a month's notice at the boarding-house. Never a pleasant thing to do. You were considered as an ungrateful wretch and treated as such, accused of idling and just seeing your time out. It never paid to tell the truth that you were going to a better job. Mum soon found this out and so did I. Sickness at home was mum's reason from then on. My excuse was always that mum had broken her leg. The number of times that accident has happened to her, particularly with charring jobs. As she says, 'I must be a blooming centipede!'

During this last month mum spent all her spare time making the necessary uniforms. All by hand; they had no sewing machine. Print dresses and those vast aprons with the long streamers on the back. It was like getting your bottom drawer filled for the wedding. And for what? To be the sort of rope in this domestic tug of war for ten pounds a year, a cubby hole in the basement (infested with beetles) as a bedroom, one afternoon off a week from three to six and alternate Sundays with the same hours. It was slave labour. Mum stuck it for two months then gave in her notice—sickness at home! According to mum nothing eventful happened at that place. If it did she doesn't remember it. It was a period of bewilderment and disillusion.

Mum had learnt one lesson about service. She was now determined that her next job would be as a kitchen-maid and in a larger establishment where her duties would be defined. She went back to the registry office and was choosey. She was able to be, because few girls wanted to be kitchen-maids. It was a job where much of your time was spent on your knees scrubbing or at the sink with your hands immersed in greasy water. The fact that you were also learning how to cook and could eventually rise to that exalted position either escaped most girls or didn't concern them. Their goal was matrimony and a less hard life on the way to the altar as it were. So mum selected a military household and went to work for a Colonel and Mrs Benson at a house in The Drive in Hove. The Colonel had of course retired. He'd been in the 17th/21st Lancers—the 'Cherrypickers' as he constantly called them. 'I don't know about him being a cherrypicker,' mum says. 'He was known in the servants' hall as a cherrypincher—he couldn't leave the housemaids' bottoms alone.' They kept a satisfactory staff as mum puts it. A butler, footman, housemaid and under-housemaid, a lady's-maid and valet, a gardener, a coachman and a stable-boy. The coachman and stable-boy lived out.

Unlike me, mother enjoyed this first job as a kitchen-maid. Everybody was so kind to her, she says, particularly the butler and the footman. Well, of course mother was a very pretty child and I reckon she must have turned on the helpless and pathetic act, though as I've known her she's never been pathetic or helpless and today can be a raging old tyrant. But she's always been a bit of an actress and a mimic. She, of course, denies that it was her looks or her manner that encouraged this sort of treatment. 'They were sorry for me because of the hard life I'd had,' she says. That's as may be, but a generation later I, a gawky, clumsy, big-footed kitchen-maid, was treated in a very condescending way particularly during the early months in my jobs.

I suppose though that our different attitudes can be ascribed to our different upbringings. I came from a home where there was love and affection. I was treated as a somebody. As the eldest girl I had to assume a lot of responsibilities. I bathed the children and put them to bed on a Saturday night when mum and dad went out to the pub for a drink. I did a lot of the shopping, particularly when mum hadn't got any money. I'd order the goods and wait till they were wrapped up and then say, 'I can't pay you now, but mum'll let you have it at the end of the week,' and scoot out as quickly as I could. During the first war I was the one who went to the soup kitchens to get a free jug of soup. I was the one who had to answer the door to the tally man who'd come to collect his money and say mum was out when she was hiding in the kitchen. I was a responsible person and respected as such. So when I went into service I was homesick and felt I was being treated as less than the dirt. For mum with an unkind, unloving home, and after two menial jobs, the slightest recognition would come as a sign of affection; and after a time when she was fully accepted as a member of the below-stairs fraternity her life by comparison would be a happy one for the first time. She looked for and found affection. I didn't look for or expect to find it inside domestic service. I got it from my own home and later on I found it outside.

Her duties were similar to mine in my first position in service but harder since the Colonel and Mrs Benson entertained very lavishly. The house, too, was often full of guests and mum would find she had to get up even earlier to light the kitchen range because more hot water was required for baths. There would be hot soup to be carried up last thing at night and a lot of extra washing up. Conditions may seem primitive by today's standards but they were not nearly so primitive if you had a staff of servants to wait on you.

Looking back on this job, mum is reminded of the lines of Kipling: 'The Colonel's lady and Judy O'Grady are sisters under the skin.' 'First impressions,' says mum, 'didn't bear this out. The Colonel's lady was an out and out snob; never noticed my presence. I can't remember her addressing two words to me in the whole time I was there. It wasn't long though before I found out she had one little weakness—she liked a lot of gin and being rich what she liked she had. Then she would become like Judy O'Grady. She'd stagger around the house swearing, knocking things over and throwing off her clothes. Often her lady's-maid used to have to put her to bed. I suppose she was what would be called today an alcoholic and we should have been sorry for her. I'm afraid we weren't. We would hear her either in our bedrooms or in the servants' hall and as far as we were concerned she was an object of shame and derision.'

It may be that the Colonel's behaviour had something to do with it. According to what the butler and the valet said his amorous behaviour didn't stop at pinching the maids' bottoms. He had a little love nest in nearby Brighton. It's amazing how much the valets got to know and from the horse's mouth as it were because apparently masters couldn't stop boasting even to their men about their amorous exploits. 'In any case I knew when he was going to visit his nest,' said his valet, 'because he'd change his underwear before he went.'

Brighton of course has always been notorious for its love nests and its hotels and for what were colloquially called dirty weekends in my younger days. It was like Paris and l'Amour; a much more glamorous sounding expression for the same thing. I suppose it all started in Brighton in the days of the Prince Regent and grew with the advent of the railway. Being by the sea perhaps the air freshened people up and made them feel frisky. There must have been more to it than that though, because Southend is near London and by the sea, and yet all it's ever been associated with is jellied eels, whelks and winkles.

Mind you, for the ordinary residents Brighton was no gayer or more sexually exotic than any other town.

Whether it was from exhaustion through his amorous exploits

or whether it was because of his wife's drinking mum doesn't know, but the Colonel often slept in a separate room from his wife. This led to a night of violence the like of which mum never before or since witnessed. The house had gone to bed. Mum was wakened from her sleep by the sound of banging and splintering wood punctuated by screamed curses. It was Mrs Benson wielding an axe on the door of the Colonel's bedroom, trying to get in. All was bedlam. The butler, the valet and the lady's-maid took their lives in their hands. They tried reasoning with her but she turned and took a blind swipe at them. 'Bloody nearly scalped the three of us,' they said later. The valet either out of loyalty to his master or to save his own skin tackled her round the legs, the butler grabbed the axe while her lady's-maid adjusted her night attire and got her to her feet. She still had to be restrained and although her arms were held she bit into the back of the valet's wrist and as he howled and let go of her she caught the butler a backhander across the nose. Eventually they got her into her room and persuaded the gallant Colonel that it was safe for him to come out of his. The housemaid went to fetch the doctor and a semblance of peace and quiet was restored. Restored that is until the next day when the servants' hall was buzzing with excitement. 'Talk about the Relief of Mafeking!' mum says. 'Compared with this that was a Sunday School party.' You see, according to the servants, the boot was on the wrong foot. A wife trying to get in to reach her husband! At that time women weren't supposed to enjoy sex, they submitted to it but they didn't look for it and as for taking an axe to get it, well! The men servants of course laughed but the women tut-tutted. She was a disgrace to their sex. They would never run after a man. As mum says, they did of course, but they thought they were doing it in a subtle way as though they were the pursued not the pursuers.

Mum says that at the time she was in a bit of a daze about it all. She didn't appreciate the implications. It was the same when I was her age. The servants used to make jokes of a sexual nature and then roar with laughter. At first I'd ask them what was so funny—this used to make them laugh even louder at my ignorance, so I gave up asking and just laughed along with them.

43

Of course the whole thing was a nine-day wonder. After a decent interval Mrs Benson came back and took charge of the household again as though nothing untoward had happened. 'And funnily enough when you looked at her you couldn't believe it had,' mum said. 'It was as though it was just a nasty dream.'

It was while mum was working at the Bensons that she saw her first horseless carriage. 'The day of the car' she constantly refers to it as. It was an event for the whole neighbourhood, and it is the way mum was allowed to behave that increases my belief that because of her looks and her manner she was given a sort of special treatment for a kitchen-maid. 'I was so excited that all morning I kept running out to see if it was on its way. I was determined not to miss it.' No cook I ever worked for would let me do that. Wasting one's time they would have called it and they would have found me a few additional chores to do to make sure I didn't leave their sight. 'I first knew it was getting near because of the noise it made and the cheers of the people watching,' mum says, 'so I shouted to the butler and all the staff assembled to watch.' Shouted to the butler indeed! As mum told me this I could imagine Mr Kite, the butler in my first place, turning over in his grave. 'The first thing to come into view was a man dressed like a coachman in leggings and gaiters, walking along in the middle of the road carrying a red flag. It was quite a considerable time after that the vehicle itself appeared. The man was there to warn people of the impending arrival of the car, but the things was chugging away so noisily that they could have heard it coming a mile away,' mum says. 'The real danger was the horses. It was a new noise to them and many of them reared up at the first sound of it. The drivers got off their carts or carriages and held the horses' heads until the thing had gone by. The dogs, too, must have hated the sound of it because every one of them in the neighbourhood was either howling or barking.'

I suppose today horses, dogs and humans have become atrophied to the frightful noise of our streeets. If they and we hadn't I suppose all of us would have had to be destroyed for the sake of progress.

44

It was the talking point in the servants' hall for days, mum says. It was the usual battle of youth versus age. The cook, butler and head housemaid all took the view that such things would die a natural death—that they were just a flash in the pan—while the under servants reckoned that they were the coming thing. The coachman, too, tried to shrug them off but mum says he went round looking gloomy for days. He probably saw them as a potential menace to his job and he knew that at his age he would have neither the ability nor the inclination to learn to handle these new monsters. The thing that was of general interest was how much the bloke who carried the flag earned and how many had had to be employed on the journey from London which was where the vehicle had come from.

One morning shortly after 'the day of the car' the servants were going about their duties before breakfast when the gardener came rushing into the kitchen and whispered something in the cook's ear. 'Oh my gawd!' she cried. 'Wait there, I'll get Mr Sims.' Mr Sims was the butler. Cook rushed off and in a few seconds returned with him and the head housemaid. Mum was told to busy herself upstairs so at the time didn't know what it was all about. She heard the story later from the under-housemaid whom she shared a bedroom with. The gardener, it appears, had just started work for the morning on one of the rose beds by the wall when he saw what he thought was a doll. He went to pick it up and to his horror saw that it was a naked new-born baby. It was dead of course, and stone cold. According to the housemaid it was whisper, whisper, whisper between the four older servants. It took them some time to decide who should tell whom upstairs. Eventually it was agreed that the head housemaid should tell Mrs Benson since they were both still in their bedroom and their room was her area of responsibility.

As it turned out the Colonel was having his bath so the housemaid was able to come out with it without its being too embarrassing. Of course Mrs Benson went off like a cannon. She exploded and screamed like mad for the Colonel who came running out with a bath towel hastily drawn round his middle. He barked out a few orders like 'Send for the police!' and 'Don't touch anything!' but, as the housemaid said, 'All pink and steaming from the bath he didn't cut a very authoritative figure.' Well by now all the household except mum was agog with excitement and mum knew that something was up but nobody would tell her what. The Colonel dressed hurriedly and went down to survey the scene while the lady's-maid was giving Mrs Benson a sniff of the smelling salts, since she'd had an attack of the vapours.

The police duly arrived and the Colonel informed them that some wretched servant girl had thrown her baby over his wall. It was straight away assumed that it was a servant girl that had done it. Not his servants of course, somebody else's. The police weren't too sure about this and after examining the body and arranging for its removal they asked the Colonel to assemble all the staff in the hall. The Colonel passed on the instructions to the butler and all of them were lined up there except mum. When the butler was asked if they were all present and correct, he said, 'Yes, sir, all that is except Florence' (my mum). 'Why isn't she here then?' asked the police and the Colonel also grunted questioningly. 'Because, begging your pardon, sir,' he said to the Colonel, 'Cook and I are of one mind in this and we do not think that a girl as innocent as Florence should be involved in this unpleasantness. Cook and I, sir, are both prepared to vouch that she could have had nothing to do with it.' That was telling them! Whether it was that staff in mum's day had a particular sense of dignity and a code of behaviour or whether it was because of mum's looks and winning ways, I don't know. All I do know is that in my time I never found any servants who would have taken it upon themselves to have made such a decision and so firmly to declare it. According to the under-housemaid they were all rigorously questioned and so were the staffs of many of the houses in the neighbourhood, but the mystery was never solved.

The incident cast a cloud over the servants' hall for a week or two, mum says, not because they suspected each other, but because of the fact that it was automatically assumed by all in authority that it was a servant's baby, that it was servant girls who had illegitimate babies and that only a servant would kill an unwanted child.

It was an important landmark in mum's life when the Colonel and Mrs Benson decided to move to Windsor and the staff were asked whether they would like to go with them. For mum it meant the final break with her home and for this reason alone she accepted, but there were other excitements to be anticipated like her first journey in a train, a fleeting glimpse of London, a new town with new shops and a different kind of people. The fact that she might see the Queen didn't bother her. In the event she never did. Exactly why the Bensons moved or who decided that they should was a matter of speculation below stairs. The valet said it was because a battalion of the Cherrypickers was doing a term of duty at the castle and although the Colonel had retired he would be able to be near some of his friends, and also together they would get involved with the social whirl that duty at the castle involved. The lady's-maid thought that the Colonel's visits to his love nest had been on the up and up and that Mrs Benson felt that more masculine company would be good for him. The valet had to agree that a lot of his underwear had been going to the laundry in recent weeks. The move was an event in itself. The Bensons left, taking the valet and the lady's-maid with them and the removal men moved in. Even today mum talks about this with an excited twinkle in her eye. I can visualise what it meant. Half a dozen new men who were nothing to do with domestic service coming to stay for a fortnight and sleeping down in the basement. All right, they may have looked scruffy and have smelt of beer and stale tobacco but to the female staff they were 'corn in Egypt'. Even the butler was amiable. He was in command of the house and the men recognised this and called him 'sir'. Although he said the Colonel had taken stock of the drink before he left he thought they could take one or two liberties with it and put it down to breakages; and they did. The men naturally enough buttered up the cook by saying they'd never tasted such cooking. What they did to the under servants or the under servants did for them mum doesn't say, but it's my bet that that twinkle wasn't in her eyes for nothing.

With the removal men came the big pantechnicons drawn by those lovely percheron horses which had to be stabled nearby. The whole move lasted about a fortnight and of course there were similar jinks when they reached Windsor, getting the stuff unloaded and the house to order.

The first journey on a train that she had so much looked forward to was exciting, but it was just a train journey. Each carriage was separate. There were no corridors so the business of going to the loo, apart from being embarrassing, because like other things it wasn't talked about quite so freely in those days, was also hazardous. You had to wait till you got to a station, then make a dash for it and hope you could make it before the train steamed off. In all other respects mum thinks that trains were more comfortable then and of course they ran on time. Railway workers were generally considered a cut above their fellows and as for a train driver—well he used the saloon bar.

The realisation of Windsor for mum didn't live up to the anticipation, she found it deadly dull and also because there was more entertaining the work was harder. She remembers seeing the schoolboys from nearby Eton and remarks on the obvious opulence of their parents. She didn't walk out with any of the soldiers, she was warned against this by the other servants; so was I, but with men being so scarce after the First World War beggars couldn't be choosers! As I've said she didn't see Queen Victoria and she didn't miss this as she never wanted to. It's funny that we think of Victorian times as being jingoistic and patriotic. It was to the upper classes, but in service your world was so small that even when you had your afternoon and evening off you didn't bother much about looking outside it. Few servants read the newspapers and none were written down to their level to encourage them. It was no different in my day. I compare it with two long spells I had in hospital. Once in hospital I lost contact with the outside world and ceased to be interested in what went on there. The hospital ward was my world and not unnaturally my interest was focused on myself. It was the same in service; I scrubbed, cleaned, washed, cooked for them upstairs and my little spare time I devoted to myself. Mostly I was so physically tired I couldn't exercise my brain.

Anyway after six boring months of Windsor mum decided she wanted a change. Because she'd been made much of by the other servants she'd lost some of her feelings of inferiority and rejection and rather looked forward to a spell with her family. She forgot that things would still be the same there. Since life was so different in service she tended to romanticise the idea of home. She was quickly disillusioned. Naturally for the journey and her home-coming she'd made herself as attractive as possible. She'd put on her best dress and to crown it she wore a straw hat trimmed with coloured pom-poms which she'd bought specially for the occasion. Her parents were at home to greet her and for the first few minutes the time passed pleasantly enough, though she could see her father's eyes from time to time surveying her hat which she'd continued to wear and his expression as he did so seemed rather derogatory. They began chatting away about the train journey and her father being an engineer started to air his knowledge. He came out with some bit of information which mum knew wasn't right and she carelessly said, 'Don't be silly, dad.' That was it. Right back to square one. He rose from his seat, snatched the hat off her head, tore off the pom-poms, put his fist through the crown and threw the lot on the fire. 'Don't you come back here with your airs and graces contradicting your elders and looking like a tart. Get up to your room and come down when you feel sorry for what you've said.' Well, that did it for mum. All right she'd nowhere to go, so she had to do as she was told, but up in her room she determined to get out as soon as possible and never come back. When mum told me this story naturally I was sympathetic, yet later I couldn't resist reminding her of the time when I was about eleven. I was sitting at home peeling the potatoes and she came up and said, 'Don't peel them so thick, you're throwing away half the potato.' I said, 'No I'm not, don't be silly, mum,' and she gave me the most awful slap across the ears. 'That was different,' she said. 'You were being purposely aggravating.' But it wasn't and I wasn't. The thing was that words had a different value in those days, possibly a real value in that they were taken as meaning what they said. To call

49

someone a fool was really to be in danger of hell fire and if someone was called a bastard it invariably led to a fight which could be justified in the eyes of the law.

The day after her return mum went to the registry office and was interviewed for and offered a job with a Colonel and Mrs Vasey in Second Avenue, Hove. A very dignified and respectable household that was. Again this Colonel had retired and both he and his wife were getting on in years. They were as different from the Bensons as chalk is from cheese. Mum says perhaps it was because he was in the Artillery, but in my experience when I was walking out with soldiers in Hyde Park their regiments were no indication of their behaviour. The Vaseys lived alone, though they had a married daughter who visited from time to time and a son who was fighting the Boers in South Africa. Mum who has lived through three wars doesn't really rate the South African war, and remembers very little about it. 'It was so far away it didn't seem real somehow. It was a story-book sort of war: George and the Dragon stuff. We heard bits about individual bravery, but we really had no idea as to why it was being fought and we thought the Boers were a lot of stupid savages not wanting to be in the Empire. We were constantly exhorted in those days to go down on our knees and thank God that we were British.' One event of the war does stand out for her because it caused her some irritation, and it concerned the Vaseys' son. Shortly after she had gone there he was killed in action. Now although mum had never seen him she was sorry for them and some of the servants who had known him were very upset. There was a sense of bereavement in the servants' hall but to everyone's astonishment and mum's utter amazement the day after his death was announced the staff were measured for mourning clothes and it was announced that the whole household would be in mourning for six months. At first mum's feelings were mixed. She was pleased to get a free dress when she could only afford to buy one a year for herself, but furious that it had to be black and that her behaviour and expression was expected to conform to it both indoors and out. Vanity I suspect played a part; mum having a brownish skin, black never did suit her.

Although because there was no body there couldn't be a funeral they did have a memorial service. This mum remembers as a very splendid affair. All the staff were assembled in the hall and as the coaches drew up were seated in them in order of precedence. The cook, butler, head housemaid and lady's-maid in the first and the under staff in the one behind. There was a procession of about twenty coaches in all. One was draped with a Union Jack, filled with flowers and wreaths and there was a sword and helmet laid on them. The service was long, mournful and impressive. None of this death on a conveyor belt that you get at crematoriums today. On their return to the house afterwards the servants were soon hustled out of any feelings of respect for the dead as they had to serve a large variety of cold collations for the living whose appetites had not been lost in the expressions of their grief.

Life afterwards was easy and uneventful, as being in mourning the Vaseys did no entertaining on a large scale. There was one thing though that happened and did cause mum to wonder and gave her feelings of unease. She had been sharing a bedroom with the under-housemaid as was usual for a kitchen-maid. One day this under-housemaid had an attack of influenza and was confined to her bed. The cook, a Mrs Melrose, the Mrs being only a courtesy title as she was in fact a spinster of some forty years, thought it best that mum moved out so that she didn't catch it and told her to shift her bed and things down to her room. Mum didn't care much for the idea but she couldn't very well refuse. This Mrs Melrose was a big woman and very tightly corsetted. Getting both in and out of them was a considerable operation, at which mum was now required to help. The getting out was accomplished with pleasurable grunts and groans and a considerable scratching. Mum was asked to assist at this latter and was given directions: 'Up a bit. Just under the shoulder. Yes that's it,' accompanied by 'OOs' and 'Ahs' of satisfaction. When this ritual was over Mrs Melrose would put on her night-gown, get on her knees and say her prayers, but all the time, mum says, her hands were scratching away as though she were covered in fleas. Then she'd leap up, go to the mirror on the chest of drawers, pick up a pair of tweezers and start tugging away on the hairs that adorned her upper lip. This was an unnecessary torture, for while it is said that two blades of grass won't grow where only one grew before she had no such difficulty with the hairs on her lip. These habits didn't appeal to mum who was fastidious, but when one night the cook climbed into bed with her she was both horrified and frightened. She lay there pretending to be asleep. Eventually Mrs Melrose went back to her own bed. The next morning she behaved as if nothing had happened and mum began to wonder if she'd been dreaming but she was scared stiff of going to bed that night. The cook had two more bouts of affection before to mum's great relief the housemaid recovered and she was able to move back into her own room.

I can't help wondering whether mum had some kind of unconscious affinity for older women. She had an attractive face and a mature body but a simplicity and innocence, either real or assumed, which appealed to their natural instincts and indeed as is apparent to deeper feelings which they themselves probably didn't understand. There was a later instance at another place where mum became very friendly with the lady's-maid. This in itself was extraordinary because although friendships did develop between a kitchen-maid and under-housemaids and under-nursemaids it was socially unacceptable between a lady's-maid and a kitchen-maid. It was against the rules. Yet it happened and was allowed by the senior staff to continue. I've seen evidence of this friendship, because when this family went abroad for the winter months the lady's-maid travelled with them and every night before she went to bed this maid wrote a page or two of a descriptive letter to mum about the places she had been to and the people she had met. Then she sewed these pages together lengthwise, rolled them up and at intervals would send this sort of documented toilet roll to mum who treasured it for years. Being in domestic service had certain similarities to being in the armed services. Both lives were hard and in both you were thrown together and kept together in small groups. It was a kind of forcing atmosphere for relationships which could grow beyond ordinary friendships into real love which in their turn demanded some kind of physical outlet.

This was an area of below-stairs morality of which employers were completely unaware, which was just as well as they spent enough time being solicitous about all the other aspects of the servants' moral and religious welfare.

Even before the Vaseys' son had been killed they had prayers in the morning before breakfast and at night after supper had been served and cleared away. Since his death these had been extended and after a hard day's work sometimes mum had difficulty in keeping awake through them. Also the Vaseys started going regularly to communion early on Sunday mornings and those of the staff that could be spared were shepherded along too. One of these mornings mum and Emily the under-housemaid were told they had to go and when they explained that they hadn't been confirmed Mrs Vasey's religious fervour was so aroused that they were sent each week to special classes at the curate's.

Although mum was furious at having religion thrust at her again she got resigned to it because she had an extra half-day off. The curate was very good-looking, he gave them tea and cakes and was prepared to listen to their chatter. 'He also had a beautiful voice,' mum says, 'and his manner was so persuasive that as he talked about heaven I'd shut my eyes and I could half imagine I was on my way up there. Then I'd open them and see him looking so masculine and handsome and I'd say to myself, "Not blooming likely, gal, who wants to go to heaven when there's lovely creatures like him on earth."'

Mum was sorry when confirmation day came round. Even more so when she got to the church because there were all the other girls, about fifty of them in lovely elaborate white dresses all specially made for the occasion and there were she and Emily rigged up in a couple of old white skirts of Mrs Vasey's that had been cut down, white school blouses and cheap white shoes. 'We may have been equal in the sight of God,' mum says, 'but in the sight of man we were what we were, a couple of skivvies.'

This really was the end of that job for mum. What with a

kinky cook, a surfeit of religion culminating in an upsurge of the old inferiority feeling that the confirmation service gave her, she'd had enough of life at the Vaseys'. So her mother 'went sick' and she gave in her notice. It's extraordinary the power employers had to direct your whole life in service. You meekly had to give way to their every whim, if you had protested you'd have been dismissed and without a reference. I suppose mum's life at the Vaseys' illustrates the truth of that saying, 'You can't even call your soul your own.'

Chapter Five

Mum was sick and tired of her religious and moral welfare so constantly being bandied about by her employers that when she came to look for another job it had to be one with a very large staff where she could live in a state of anonymity, at any rate as far as those upstairs were concerned. Although like me she is no real lover of the country now, then she had more sentimental ideas about it and fancied a place in a country house. She got one, again as a kitchen-maid, to a Lord Jissin, VC. He lived outside Chichester at Bosham. She arranged it so that she left the Vaseys and went straight to this new job thus avoiding going back home to stay even for a night or two. Not unnaturally mum was on very friendly terms with most of the trades people and when one of them heard she was going to Bosham he offered to run her over there in his small horse and cart. This was a great adventure for mum. When I suggested to her that she was taking a bit of a risk she said, 'What do you mean?' I explained that she couldn't have known him all that well and that he might have taken advantage of the situation to have his way with her. 'Stuff and nonsense, gal. People didn't act that way in those days. The thought never entered my head and I'm sure it didn't enter his. We had a lovely ride sitting side by side with my old tin trunk rattling away on the cart.' The tradesman dropped mum at Lord Jisson's lodge gates about two o'clock. The lodge keeper's wife came out to meet her and explained that she'd arrived too early. 'They won't be expecting you till four and you'll only be in the way up there, so you'd best stay here and Mr Baines (her husband) will take you up later in the trap.' Apparently in those sort of places four o'clock was the time appointed for staff to arrive and they weren't expected to be early or late. While she was waiting mum learned quite a bit from Mrs Bains. Lord Jisson lived in this great house alone. He was married but his wife lived abroad because she enjoyed ill health. Mum says she said this bit about Lady Jisson rather darkly, so later did others of the staff but there was never a breath of scandal about her, it was just that she was a mystery to them and remained so until mum left. His Lordship enjoyed the typically British life of the time, hunting, shooting and fishing. He had no other interests and though he entertained, his guests were only people who enjoyed similar pursuits. He kept his own pack of hounds and was of course Master of the Hunt. He kept an indoor and outdoor staff of over forty servants all to tend to his needs. Mum tentatively enquired about his church-going habits. To her relief it appeared he wasn't particularly religious and didn't interfere in this matter with the members of his staff, but of course had his own pew in the church where, because he was a local JP, he had to put in an appearance from time to time. By the time Mr Baines was ready to take her to the big house mum was quite cheerful about the job and confident that she'd made the right choice.

As they drove up the drive her confidence began to wane. It was a long way, well over a mile and the house didn't even come into view until they had gone halfway. The trees seemed to get bigger and bigger and mum, like Alice, felt smaller and smaller. 'When eventually I saw the house I could understand about the forty servants. It was an enormous building with pillars and long wide steps, surrounded by masses of stables and outbuildings. It was a world all of its own. It began to seem as though I was going into a prison and I got dead scared. I think Mr Baines must have realised this because he patted my hand and said, "Don't worry, gal, it isn't as bad as it looks." Eventually he drove round to the servants' entrance, dumped my trunk by the door, pulled one of those clanging bells and left me to my fate. One of the under-housemaids let me in, helped me with my trunk and then took me into the servants' hall. They were having tea. What looked like hundreds of eyes turned on me then turned away again and their owners carried on talking as though I didn't exist, though some of them glanced at me from time to time as I drank the cup of tea that had been put in front of me. I felt terrible. Talk about "Little Orphan Annie"! All my old inferiority came surging back. Eventually someone suggested I be shown where I was going to sleep and the same under-housemaid whom I had to share a room with, took me, helping me carry my trunk upstairs. The room was all right; I unpacked, changed into my uniform and made my way downstairs again to the servants' hall. The cook was now there. She'd been out for the afternoon and I was sort of shown to her. She grunted and told me to sit down out of the way and when she'd finished what she was doing she'd take me to see the housekeeper. I'd met the housekeeper before, but it's one thing being interviewed in a registry office and quite another when you're actually in the job.'

I know exactly how mum felt—unwanted. One thing I could never understand was the other servants' attitudes. They were always so unfriendly and in your early days they would make fun of you and jeer at you, yet they must have been through the same experience themselves and then longed for a friendly word and some sympathetic understanding. The upper servants of course were tarred with the same brush as their employers. Theirs was just as rigid a hierarchy and they wouldn't lower themselves to speak familiarly with a kitchen-maid, but it wouldn't have hurt the under servants to make some sort of kind gesture. I know I did as I got higher up the domestic ladder. In fact I was reprimanded by one of my employers who told me I'd never make a good cook as I was too kind to the under servants. I never could understand how my kindness was likely to transfer itself and spoil the food they were served with.

Eventually the cook finished whatever it was she was doing and mum was taken to the 'Pug's Parlour'. This was the servants' nickname for the housekeeper's room. It was a universal name although sometimes it was abbreviated to 'The Puggery'. No one has been able to tell me how it originated or where or when, but it persisted even to when I was in service. It was the housekeeper's room and in it the butler, valet and lady's-maid ate with her. The cook superintended the meals in the servants' hall but when it came to the sweet course she and the head house-maid took their plates into the Puggery and were allowed to eat it there. It was a rigid rule. When I look at advertisements now-adays and see—'Required butler–chauffeur–handyman', I can imagine some of the butlers I served under, turning in their graves. Such a combination of duties! All they were required to do was 'buttle' but they did this to perfection. I heard from a friend recently who works in one of these country places. There's a Polish butler, an Indian footman, Spanish and Portuguese housemaids, a French chef and an Italian gardener. 'Talk about the United Nations,' she says. 'Nobody understands a word the others are saying, yet they're all screaming away at the same time.'

Mum got her list of duties from the housekeeper who was prompted from time to time by the cook. What struck her as being funny was that she was not only told what she'd got to do but what she hadn't got to do. This house was run on strictly military principles. There were things expected of you and things expected of others and never the twain must overlap. Come to think of it, it's very like the unions, although of course unions were hardly thought of then. I believe that if there'd been one started for domestic servants there might be a lot more people working in service now because if it had been played to certain rules and given a social standing it could have been a worthwhile job and a first-class training for life. Some people still believe it was, but they are mainly the erstwhile employers.

After seeing the housekeeper and cook mum went back to the kitchen. Cook's attitude towards her had warmed somewhat; she'd gathered that mum was experienced. She showed her where all the necessary utensils were and mum was relieved that at last she was looked on as a person and was not just sitting around like a spare unwanted part.

It seems extraordinary that though she was at Lord Jisson's for nearly two years mum isn't able to describe the inside of the house. She knew the hall and she had a glimpse into the rooms leading off it, but she never went into them. It wasn't her place to, as she says. She never went up the main staircase and never saw a bedroom. The hall became very familiar because she had to scrub it each day, and an arduous task it was because the field sports that his Lordship and his friends indulged in meant muddy boots tramping in and out. It had a mosaic floor which made it even more difficult to clean and there were Persian rugs scattered around which also took considerable punishment from the boots. The walls were hung with oil paintings of battle scenes and ugly men in uniforms, sort of ancestors mum supposed. These were interspersed with antlers, lions' and tigers' heads and foxes' heads and tails. 'You had to call the tails brushes in the country otherwise people laughed at you,' mum says. These were the spoils of the chase. Despite their horrible expressions mum used to feel sorry for them. She never could get used to fox-hunting. She hated the idea, though of course she didn't have the courage or the stupidity to express her views. She could identify her own life with that of the fox and used to have nightmares imagining herself being chased by the hounds. 'Fanciful creature I was in those days,' she sniffs now, as though she is ashamed of her weakness. One job mum was spared, and that was scrubbing the steps. This was done by the boot-boy once a week and it took him a whole day they were so long and wide, but he had to brush and wipe them down each day. This boot-boy was both a bane and a delight in mum's life. He was always playing tricks on her, jumping out and frightening her when she was walking down dark passages, but, and probably because they were the lowest of the low in the domestic caste system, they became very friendly. This Clarence (which even in those days was a dangerous name to have in service and which led to his being nicknamed Clara much to his fury) was only thirteen years old, but like many boys who came from hard homes he seemed much older and he was very pert. He was constantly cheeking the other servants but got away with murder because of his age. Nevertheless he had to work harder than any of the others because his duties weren't so rigidly defined and he was at the beck and call of all the upper staff.

When she had finished serving meals to the other servants he and mum used to have theirs together. Then this Clarence would chat to mum and tell her of the dreadful revenge he was going to wreak on the various people whom he considered had wronged him. The butler in particular was in for a very rough time if Clarence had his way. His voice and his gestures were so horrifying that sometimes mum had difficulty swallowing her food. If ever conversation lapsed they used to pass the time listening to the crickets which would sometimes jump right across the room and on to their table. This in my experience is a rarity because I found they only ever came out at night.

This boot-boy's duties, unlike the other servants', didn't stop when he went to bed at night. He was night-watchman and had to rig up his bed in the butler's pantry in front of the silver safe. This was a huge affair. You could walk around it and imagine you were in Ali Baba's cave. But what that poor boy used to imagine at night lying there alone with everyone else at the top of the house mum didn't like to think. If anyone did break in it would have been an easy job to silence him. Still each morning when mum went down he was cheerful enough. Once he did play a trick on mum—she found him on his face stretched out on the floor to all events and purposes dead. She let out a terrible scream and ran upstairs yelling murder all the way and woke the whole house up. Clarence never tried that trick again.

The food that was cooked and served there was out of this world, mum says. The kitchen range was enormous and all the bread for the house was baked in the ovens. The sirloins and the saddles they cooked were so heavy that mum could hardly lift them. The beef dripping spread on the home-baked bread would be a meal in itself today, mum says. The game and poultry were roasted on a revolving spit which was worked by a sort of clock-work mechanism. Mum can't stand game now and she thinks her antipathy dates back to this time when she was endlessly having to pluck and clean the birds and skin the hares all of which had been hung until they reeked to high heaven. And except when

60

Lord Jisson entertained all this was done for one man. The staff naturally fed well but even so an awful lot went to waste, although probably the pigs didn't think so. Beer was also part of the staple diet. It was ordered by the butler on his own authority direct from the brewers. Each of the servants was allowed two glasses a day, one at midday and one after supper and this included the boot-boy. Like the beer at Shoreham this did a lot for you, says mum, and it gave ideas to the men servants. When I asked her to elaborate on this she wouldn't but her eyes got a reminiscent twinkle. Although mum had a taste for beer she used to save some of hers for the organ grinder who visited twice a week. This seemed a long haul just to play for impecunious servants, but apparently Lord Jisson was fond of this sort of music and made it worth his while. The servants alone made it worth while even if they had little money; he was always given a good meal and there were fruit and tit bits for his monkey too. It was his being a touch of the outside world that made him so welcome as much as the music he played, mum reckons.

Being near the sea there was always plenty of fresh fish being regularly delivered. Lord Jisson had his own oyster beds and of course it was mum's job to open the oysters. It's a wretched task and hazardous until you get used to it, but once you have it's almost as easy as shelling peas. Mum had read some story about a servant maid having found a magnificent pearl in an oyster which had made her fortune, so being of an imaginative and optimistic nature she always looked for a quiet corner to open them in the hope that something similar would happen to her. It's easy now to laugh at this dreaming, but like mum I found it helped me to get through many of the more miserable chores.

Mum was now beginning to realise that there were certain drawbacks in being too attractive as a kitchen-maid. While it was flattering and satisfying to have the men servants paying attention to you and fussing over you, this aggravated the women who were generally in a position to make life difficult for you if they wanted to. It was a delicate tightrope to walk and wasn't made any easier for her when the butler, Mr Porter, started to take a fancy to her. This in itself was extraordinary and in the

61

normal way a thing that couldn't have happened. Mr Porter was married and he and his wife and six daughters lived in a cottage on the estate. He very much wanted a son, partly, mum thinks, to carry on the family tradition since both his father and his grandfather before him had been butlers. Anyway Mrs Porter got pregnant again and mum being soft-hearted offered to go and help with the house and children in her spare time. Naturally she became friendly with the family and this relationship Mr Porter carried over to their work. Mum says there was nothing in it, but then this twinkle comes into her eye. 'He said I'd got ears like pink seashells,' she says. Well, I reckon that saying that then was like asking someone to shack up with you in this permissive age. Then she tells me he used to follow her when she went down the cellars to draw the beer and that's not exactly a job that two can do better than one. Finally she says that she asked him for a photograph. Well, if that wasn't the 'Open Sesame' to the greatest of all treasures at that time I don't know what was. 'He refused,' mum says. Well, of course he did. Imagine mum with a photo of the butler on her chest of drawers. As it was she was foolish enough. She confided in the under-housemaid. Confided in! It was like giving the town crier news of the death of the monarch. It was all over the servants' hall in an instant; and of course there was a lot of spite in the remarks that were bandied around. It was a difficult time for mum but she managed to survive it. It was interesting that eventually when Mrs Porter had her child it was yet another girl. He was very disconsolate and not to be comforted when the cook said, 'Well you've proved yourself again. It's only a dominant male that has girls.' Then somewhat maliciously she said, 'What are you going to call her— Florence?'

Although it was the under-housemaid who'd let the cat among the pigeons by spreading the gossip about mum and the butler, she was always mum's closest friend at Lord Jisson's. Her name was Rowena and she was called by it which shows how democratic that house was. Women servants as a rule were not allowed to have names that were out of the ordinary, indeed it was the first time that Rowena had been able to use her real Christian name in service. It again shows the kind of consideration they were generally given; common names for common people.

This Rowena, mum says, was one of the plainest girls she'd ever met. Her hair was a rusty gingery colour, she didn't seem to have any eyebrows or eyelashes, she had fat dumpy cheeks and a squat shapeless figure, yet she was always going on to mum about men and their fiendish ways. I found this too; the plainer they came the more they seemed to know. I used to think opportunity would be a fine thing! It appeared that Rowena had a sister called Maud who'd been a nursemaid; this in itself was one up the social ladder for Rowena basking in her sister's reflected glory. Walking the baby in the park one day Maud was accosted by a handsome gentleman, a man of real class, said Rowena, and he, on the pretence of admiring the infant, ended by admiring the nursemaid. Maud was besieged by him and, as the song puts it, ended up in his garden with him where he seduced her and got her with child. A commonplace enough story but its importance to Rowena was that a gentleman should not only have fancied her sister but have had his way with her. It was a sexual oneupmanship. Mum expecting some sort of sorry ending with a moral in the tail for her benefit listened for the pay off. It never came. Of course the gentleman discarded Maud but one of his relations adopted the child and set Maud up in a glove shop in London. Sort of new gloves for old cast off ones.

Rowena must have been of the adventurous type because some years later she called on mum and told her that after leaving Lord Jisson she got a job through an agency as a head housemaid in the United States. Apparently the people she was employed by were more impressed by the fact that she'd worked for a real lord than they were by her experience and references. She painted a glowing picture of domestic life as lived in America. Servants were always addressed by their Christian names and called their employers Mr or Missis—none of the sirs and madams. Outings were liberal and you didn't have to account for where you'd been or get in at a particular time. They actually practised equality. There was none of this all-being-equal-in-the-sight-of-the-Lord-but-you're-not-in-heaven-yet kind of attitude that there was here.

Still the system didn't work, at any rate as far as white servants were concerned. The trouble was, Rowena said, that as you began to feel equal to the people you were working for and waiting on, you said to yourself if I am equal why am I waiting on you. She was going back to the States but as a supervisor in a shop. There's a moral in this somewhere but I'm not sure what.

Although mum never saw over the house she got to know the grounds like the back of her hand. During the spring and summer she'd wander through the fields and explore the woods and coppices. There was no fear of her being accosted since they were closely guarded by gamekeepers. Pheasants and partridges were reared in great numbers and it was wonderful to watch them grow into such beautiful creatures. It made the plucking and drawing of them so much worse, mum says. They looked so proud and free in the woods and such sorry things hanging in rows by their necks.

Naturally mum became quite friendly with the gamekeepers and their families and would often visit them in their homes. In the country they were as unpopular with the locals as policemen were in towns—even the wives and children were treated coldly —but they were generally respected. If a gamekeeper walked into a pub there was often a moment or two of silence and then conversation would be resumed but on a very different level. They used to tell mum a lot of terrifying stories about poachers and because they came from a long line of gamekeepers there would be stories passed down by their forebears of man traps, booby traps and tortures practised on poachers, and the terrible sentences that used to be meted out to them by the local justices. The JPs had gone soft nowadays, they said, and mum is sure they would have liked to see the death penalty brought back for stealing game. It was nothing even then for a man to be shot in the woods and although the gamekeeper was charged it was only a formality. He'd say he thought it was a fox in the bushes and since the victim had no business to be there the gamekeeper always got let off by the magistrates without even a caution. They were on his side to a man.

Mum says that they were not really hard men. It was their job to rear the birds and they were judged on the kind of shoot they were able to produce. If it was a poor one their vigilance was in question and they were in danger of getting the sack. It was their pride in their work and the security of their jobs and home that dictated their behaviour.

It was when things got a bit warm between her and the butler that mum acquired her first regular boy friend. Whether it was a sort of double bluff or not is a matter for speculation. All women are close about intimate details of their men, but mothers can be even more secretive with their daughters even when their ages are ninety-one and sixty-four respectively. Information has to be winkled out and there has to be a certain amount of surmise in the light of these behaviour patterns, which sounds a bit psycho-analytical; something I've tried to avoid being about mum. Anyway this boy friend was called Ernest, not a name I like, it's got a quality connotation that has never appealed to me in people. He was about thirty which considering mum was only eighteen was a big age gap for the time and particularly for her first boy friend. I was always a bit suspicious of older men. I wondered what they'd been doing all this time and it struck me as a bit suspicious that they hadn't got married before. It sort of set me on the lookout for any chinks in their armour. Ernest was a clerk in Lord Jisson's estate office. He was considered a great con-quest by the other servants; a white-collar worker was a real step up the ladder for anyone in service. Also when he came to collect mum on her evenings off he wore a suit with tight-fitting drain-pipe trousers, a jacket to match and a sober-coloured tie. 'Dressed up to the nines he was,' mum says. 'He also took snuff, a foul habit, there were always little spots of it up his nostrils and on his moustache.' How mum got close enough to observe this I didn't bother to ask. Courting was easier in the summer than in the winter apparently; it took the form of walking in the fields and woods hand in hand or occasionally Ernest would venture an arm round mum's waist. In the winter there were various 'dos' on at the village hall, lantern slide lectures, and on Sundays there'd be the PSA concerts, short for 'Pleasant Sunday After-noon', where people sang ballads and sacred music. Occasionally mum was allowed to bring him into the kitchen and they'd sit looking at each other and saying nothing because there wasn't anything to say. Talking about the good old days, it seems that people really were good then! In between meetings Ernest would send mum little notes extolling the beauty of nature and comparing her with flowers and things. This was the nearest they seem to have got to sex. The next step would have been writing or talking about the birds and the bees, I suppose. Came the day when Ernest invited mum to his home to meet his mother. When that happened it was assumed that you were courting regular and it was considered a preliminary to the engagement and the altar steps. The mother was a widow and therefore presumably dependent on her son's money so mum got a very cool reception. Mum wasn't that much put out as she wasn't taking the affair seriously. According to her she only allowed it to continue because she was flattered a clerk should be interested in her and that she was the envy of the other servants. Anyway whether it was that she was finding Ernest's attentions tedious, or the butler situation was getting out of hand, or whether it was, as she says, that being in the country was getting her down, mum decided to leave Lord Jisson's. Also she decided to see if she could better herself, so she added two years to her age and wrote off in reply to an advertisement for a good plain cook. Now the job of a plain cook, good, bad or indifferent, meant that you went to a household where they kept the minimum of staff and although you were called a cook you also had to continue the duties of kitchen-maid and you might also have to do certain other jobs around the house. Nevertheless it was a cut above being head kitchen-maid even in a big country house. To her surprise mum was interviewed and got the job. It was for a Jewish family called Jacobs. He owned a big jeweller's shop in Brighton and a house in the The Drive. Mum was quite ignorant of Jewish ways and customs and was bewildered by the various taboos associated with their religion and the utensils they used for meals, the different washing up bowls and the various tea cloths. Then there was the fish frying marathon on Fridays; enough fish was cooked to last the week. How it kept so well surprised her even with cool larders and fresh ice every day. There were two other servants, a house-maid and a parlourmaid, each of whom had charge of her own domain so that mum didn't give orders; on the other hand she didn't have to take them from anyone except Mrs Jacobs. Neither of the other servants was Jewish. It's extraordinary neither mum nor I have ever come across any Jewish servants and between us we've been in a number of jobs. As a race I don't think they're cut out for it for which I don't blame them. At first Mrs Jacobs was in and out of the kitchen instructing mum on kosher cook-ing and of course the servants had to eat the same kind of food. The thing they all missed was bacon, but as Mrs Jacobs's visits grew rarer mum was able to come to some arrangement with the grocer who slipped her a pound of bacon from time to time and charged it up as something else. I asked her what she fried it in. She winked and said, 'What the eye doesn't see the heart doesn't grieve over.' The feast of the Passover was a rough time below stairs. Everything in the kitchen had to be washed, the walls, the china, the cupboards, and not a crumb or crust of food had to be left. They were very observant about their sabbath and their holy days and never did any kind of work at all. I remember when I was about ten years old I used to earn a copper or two a week by going round and lighting the fires for some Jewish people on a Saturday morning. They were kind and generous and they always offered me sweets and things. It was all right for 'goys' to break their sabbath. If you worked for Christians even though you were a disbeliever you had to keep theirs and in their way.

Although mum thought that by taking this job in Brighton she would be able to make a break with Ernest she was wrong. He did indeed live up to his name. Shortly after she'd started at the Jacobses' there was a knock at the back-door, she opened it, and there he was drain-pipe trousers and all, holding a bunch of flowers. It turned out he couldn't stand life without her so he'd given up his job on the estate and was now working as a clerk for the Southern Railway in Brighton. Well, of course mum was flabbergasted and dismayed yet flattered. The feeling flattered bit dropped off as the weeks went by and eventually she plucked up her courage and told him that she could never marry him. She had to think of some excuse to soften the blow and she had an inspiration. 'It's that mother of yours,' she said. 'I know she thinks I'm inferior and she makes me feel it.' Ernest said that they would live away from her, but mum said she knew that would never work. She was adamant, Ernest went away heart-broken, and mum thought that that was that. But it wasn't. A few days later there was a ring at the back-door and there was Ernest's mother as large as life and twice as loud. She laid into mum about how she with her lies had come between mother and son and broken up their happy household. It turned out that Ernest had gone back and repeated everything that mum had said, had packed up his belongings and had gone she knew not where. The way she went on, mum said, you'd have thought mum had seduced her son and left an illegitimate baby on her doorstep. It seems to me in those days they had all the drama without any of the fun. Eventually of course Ernest's mother left and that at last was the end of that, but mum in reminiscent mood often wistfully wonders what ever became of her Ernest.

It taught her a lesson, she says, because Mr Jacobs turned out to be a frisky Romeo of fifty who whenever his wife was out was continually going down into the kitchen and chatting her and the parlourmaid up. 'He'd stand with his hands in his pockets rattling away at his money and ask whether he could meet us on our days off. I quickly told him that I always had to go home to my sick parents,' mum says. 'The parlourmaid wasn't so sensible, she did go out with him, only once, but that was enough. One of Mrs Jacobs's friends saw him and reported back. Well, the up-roar that went on. It made my "to do" with Ernest's mother seem like a friendly sort of argument,' mum says. The parlour-maid was sacked on the spot and the house shook for days as the battle continued. Eventually things got back to normal, but they'd not long settled down before Mr Jacobs was back in the kitchen again with a pair of slippers which he said he'd give mum if she'd let him put them on. 'Men never seem to learn,' mum says. 'They were lovely slippers but he never did give them to me.'

Apart from this battle royal mum found the Jacobses very

highly emotional. The Jews I worked for were the same. They held the family unit as something very dear and showered love and affection on their children, the next moment they were screaming at them for their base ingratitude so that you thought they had become bitter enemies for life, then the next they were all friendly as though nothing had been said. I liked working for them and so did mum. They were so highly colourful and they made servants feel part of the family, even though they saw to it that you worked very hard.

Mum was sorry to leave them. Her reason for doing so was irrational against the background of her life up till then, but it shows that Jewish people are not alone in feeling the magnetism of their families.

Chapter Six

One Sunday afternoon, just after mum had finished clearing away the lunch things, one of her younger brothers came to the back-door and told her her mother was ill and would she go back home and see her. Being a Sunday mum was able to get out without asking permission. When she arrived home she found it wasn't her mother who wanted to see her but her father. Her mother had been taken out by another brother. It appeared that some time back her mother had had some funny turns, sort of fainting fits. At first her father said they didn't take much notice as she was approaching 'a certain age', which was the way people had then of describing the change of life in a woman. However, after one rather bad attack she had to take to her bed for a few days and when she got up she started acting peculiarly: talking to herself and laughing at nothing in particular. Then she took to getting up in the middle of the night and doing the housework. Mum's father called the doctor in, who wasn't much help. He prescribed some medicine for her and said she'd either get better or worse. She got worse. One morning she got up early and left the house. When her two sons went to work, they were both employed at the same place, their foreman looked astonished to see them. 'Your mum was around earlier,' he said, 'and told me you were both ill and wouldn't be coming.' Well, naturally they were surprised; they didn't say anything to the foreman, but told their dad when they got back home. He decided least said, soonest mended, but it wasn't, because about two weeks later their mother disappeared again in the morning, and this time had told their foreman that they were fed up with him and the job and were packing it in. Well, of course this time there was more explaining to be done and to hint that your mother was going a bit peculiar was neither nice nor profitable, since insanity was thought to run in the family and any future mistakes on their part might get queer looks from their mates, as naturally this sort of news was passed round quickly. That night, when the boys got home, they had some heated words with their father.

As mum learned later from her brother, they argued late into the night. The suggestion that she should be asked to return home came up early but her father was against asking her. He felt it meant him eating humble pie and he wasn't the sort of man to do that. There were no other female relations on either side of the family who'd be able to do it. Neighbours might have helped but they were ruled out immediately. Nobody at that time wanted neighbours to know their business and this was a particularly nasty business. Eventually it was narrowed down to either her going into an asylum or asking mum back home. If she had gone to the asylum everybody would have known. It was a greater social slur than the workhouse. She'd have been referred to as a looney, being barmy, off her crumpet, having bats in the belfry or rats in the attic and all these expressions would have been visited on her family. Mental illness was a thing to laugh and sneer at. Not because people were particularly malicious, but because it was something that they couldn't understand and were afraid of. There was nothing for it, father had to swallow his pride, but he got one of the boys to ask mum to the house.

After her father had explained the situation, he had to put the question to mum, 'Would she come back home, run it and look after himself, the boys and her mother?' Without any hesitation mum said that she would. 'When could she come?' Mum said that she would speak to the Jacobses. She didn't think they would insist on her seeing her notice out. She was right. When she explained the position, Mrs Jacobs said that her place was with her family, she could leave immediately, that she herself would do the cooking until they got a replacement, and mum

71

was given a month's wages as a present. Kind, generous people, the Jews.

I'm afraid I'm not so kind or so generous. I've said to mum many times how I wasn't able to see why she went back. She'd been cruelly treated by both her parents. There was no question of blood being thicker than water because they weren't her mother and father. She was doing well in service, leading a comparatively happy life, she'd lost her feeling of inferiority, yet she was prepared to surrender herself knowing full well that within a few weeks the sacrifice she'd made would be forgotten, and she'd be treated once again as a piece of furniture. Her reply has always been the same, that at that time there could be no question as to what she would do. She saw it as her duty. It seems you were born with certain obligations and if called upon you carried them out, regardless of any circumstances. It was tradition. There were many variations of it. I had a friend, an attractive woman, who'd had many offers of marriage, but she felt she couldn't leave her widowed mother. 'She needs me, she would die of loneliness if I left her, she's told me so.' The sting is in the tail. 'She told me so.' It's like that other remark mothers make about would-be boy friends: 'We don't want any outsiders do we, dear, it's so cosy with just our two selves.' Unfortunately the situation ultimately begs the question; 'Who is going to look after those who have done the looking after?'

It turned out to be as mum had anticipated. Her mother, in her sane moments, behaved as harshly as ever towards her. She also resented that mum had the running of the house, although, as mum says, she did everything in her power to make it look as though she was just carrying out her mother's instructions. Again here, I would have thought, was a chance for mum to get a bit of her own back. She didn't. She was sorry for her mother and never once harked back to the days when she was hounded and ill-treated, never attempted to point out the sacrifices she was making in return for a loveless childhood. I suppose that is why when I and my brothers and sisters occasionally moan at mum for something she did to us as children, she gets so upset. Ours is a different kind of thinking and yet we had a happy home life.

Her father did now treat her with a kind of respect, as though she was a responsible person. He didn't talk to her much, but he didn't criticise what she was doing or the way she did it. He was more subdued. He obviously disliked the change in his wife, but he was sorry for her. Occasionally he would fly into a rage when he came home to find she'd pulled the blinds down, stuffed books under the rugs, stopped the clocks or some equally irrational things, but when he recovered he'd bury his face in his hands as if he were blaming himself for his lack of understanding. Mum thinks that her mother was lucky. Few working-class men would have behaved with the same restraint, and many would have tried to beat sense into her. Her two younger brothers she didn't see much of. She made them their packed lunches and gave them their dinner when they came home, after which they went out. They treated the house as if it was leprous. The two elder sons, who were married, never came near. Mum thinks it was their wives who kept them away in case they should be called upon to do something for their mother-in-law.

Just as her mother's mental aberrations had started, so it seems they ended. She became completely rational again and with the agreement of her father, mum found another job. She wanted something impersonal, just in case she was called upon to go back home again, so when the job of cook at a private school was offered her, she took it. It was a boarding establishment with some thirty pupils, between the ages of seven and thirteen, run by two middle-aged spinsters. While the children weren't ill-treated in any way, they were half starved physically and intellectually. There was nothing mum could do for them physically, she couldn't make their rations stretch any further. It was half everything. Half a slice of bacon, half a boiled egg, one sausage with mashed potato, watery porridge just to make it look more, half a kipper on Sundays. It sounds like a slimming diet, not meals for growing children. The two spinsters did the teaching, and what they knew, mum reckons, could have been written on the back of a postage stamp. They advertised themselves as having been governesses to the gentry, which, mum says, may have been true but they must have got found out. Mum felt sorry for them, they were such pathetic creatures, but she was sorrier for the children. Most of them were permanent boarders with parents working abroad in places that were unsuitable for children. Even if they'd been at the North Pole, mum thinks it would have been better for them to have been with their mothers and fathers.

Apparently though they weren't pathetic all the time. They would get up to the usual childish tricks, like putting mice in her and the housemaid's beds, creeping up behind her and tying the strings of her apron in knots, even dropping slugs into her mixing bowl, though they must have known this meant even less food. There was an air of faded gentility over the whole place. Mum stuck it for six months and was just beginning to wonder how she could leave without upsetting the old ladies; she didn't like to use the excuse that her mother was ill in case this time it might come true; she'd got superstitious about it. Then it happened: her mother did become ill, and she got another call to go home.

This time she had taken to her bed and refused to leave it, which was disastrous for the men of the house. The doctor had been called in again, and said there was nothing organically wrong with her, but that unless she was persuaded to leave her bed, she might stay there for the rest of her life. 'A blooming medical genius that man,' says mum. 'And he charged for saying it!'

Anyway apart from running the house, she had the job of coaxing her mother out of bed, 'Which was often more trouble than it was worth,' says mum. 'She was out of harm's way when she was between the sheets. When she was around the house I never knew what she'd be up to.' It took her mother much longer to get sufficiently well to run the house again. Before mum left, the doctor came. 'She'll never be the same woman again,' he said wisely. 'Hardly to be expected, having had the change of life,' mum thought. 'But,' he went on, 'I think it would be good for her to take up the reins again. You've done a very good job, Florence,' he added patronisingly, pocketing his five shillings.

Mum decided to be optimistic about her mother's future and

got a proper position as cook, to a Mrs Stafford in Hove. The job was recommended to her by the dustman, who was keeping company with the housemaid there. This was to be the happiest place mum had. Mrs Stafford was a pleasure to work for. She treated her servants almost as friends, and as no one took advantage of this mum really had the feeling of belonging to a happy family at last. She got twenty pounds a year, not a lot of money, but there wasn't a large staff, just a cook, housemaid, parlourmaid, coachman, gardener and nanny. This nanny's name was Fanny Fayre, which sounds unbelievable but I can personally vouch for the truth of it because I met her. She had three children to look after, two young girls and a baby son, who was the Staffords' pride and joy. Even Fanny Fayre was easy to get on with, mum says, which is amazing, as there was traditionally always a feud between cooks and nannies. As I've said, it was through the Staffords that I had my first contact with mum's working life before she was married. It's one of my earliest recollections. When my dad was out of work, mum used to go there to help out, and sometimes my brothers and I were taken along. We had to sit quietly in the kitchen, while mum got on with her job. By then a great tragedy had happened in the house. Their son, who had always been rather a sickly child, had developed consumption, and of course in those days it was almost always incurable. I remember him as beautiful-looking, a strange expression to use about a boy. He, too, was very friendly with the servants. Although I wasn't told he was probably dying, I sensed there was something different about him. It was from the way everyone treated him, with a kind of respectful sadness as though he was already half an angel. I remember, too, thinking, 'Mum never talks to us in that tone of voice,' and wondering why she didn't. It was funny, too, I thought, that when he died and although everyone knew he was going to, it was a greater calamity than if someone in perfect health had suddenly dropped dead.

Consumption was then, as cancer is today, a dread disease. I had an uncle who lost his wife from it and later his two daughters.

Mum found the other two indoor servants were also very easy to get on with, probably, she thinks, because they were both courting and could see the end of domestic service. But when she told me that one had been engaged for ten years and the other for fifteen, all I could say was that they must have been long-sighted. Although mum liked working there, the living conditions for the servants were bad. The kitchen was like a cellar and was under the conservatory and the garden. There were no windows at all, just a panel of thick green glass in the ceiling which went clickerty-clack as people in the conservatory walked over it. In the summer they did get a chink or two of light through it, but they worked by gas-light day and night. There was the usual kitchen range and dozens of copper saucepans. I wondered how all the work could be done with so few servants. Mum says Mrs Stafford seemed to collect a lot of odd people who came in from time to time to help. For example there was a Mr Hungerford, who came once a month to clean the six chandeliers. Mum says he approached his job with reverence, as though he was dealing with diamonds. He'd unhook each piece of glass, clean it with methylated spirits and then polish it till it shone. If he could have seen the way she was to clean them later—plunging the whole thing into a sinkful of soapy water, then running cold water over them—he'd have fainted right out. Still I must say hers always looked bright and shining. I suppose it's all a question of degree.

Mr Hungerford's hobby was genealogy. He showed mum a copy he'd made of his family tree. This was supposed to explain that the Hungerfords had been the backbone of some village since time immemorial. Mum really couldn't have cared less if they'd been kings of England. She just chatted to him for company and while he was talking she used to gaze at him in wonderment to think that this man of a height of no more than five feet, with a bald head, bulbous eyes, receding chin, had had three wives and had sired numerous little Hungerfords, twigs to the family tree. It's often the case though, that the most unlikely material produces the results. I know, I've been out with innocuous-looking boy friends who've talked about their mother and sisters, the vicar and Bible classes, only to find when they got me into the cinema, they'd as many hands as an Indian Buddha and the singleness of purpose of an Everest climber. It works in reverse too. I once went out with a bloke with the looks of Clark Gable and the figure of Hercules, but all his goods were in the shop window. He had no hidden attributes, or if he did he didn't exercise them. He'd spent all his time getting a body he'd never learnt how to use.

Another of Mrs Stafford's band of irregulars was old Clara, who came every morning to clean the steps and the brasses. She'd originally worked for Mrs Stafford's grandmother as a house-maid, and had been handed down as an heirloom. She was now a toothless old crone, sucking away at a dirty clay pipe, taking it out and spitting at intervals with the accuracy of a cowhand from the West. Mum remembers Clara describing a railway journey she took shortly after the line from London to Bristol had been opened. The family she had been working for had rented a house at Bath for the summer so they took the servants with them. They had a first-class carriage, and the servants travelled third. When they heard about it, the staff were thrilled with the idea of this new adventure, but when they arrived at the station they found that third class meant travelling in open trucks. In the excitement this didn't worry them as they got in, but after the train had started and rain began to fall, their excitement turned to anger. They'd also put on their best clothes for the occasion, which not only got drenched but covered in black smuts from the engine. They refused to go back the same way, which in those days was tantamount to mutiny. They won the day though and travelled second class for the return journey. According to Clara, it was very comfortable in second-class carriages, so much so that the well-to-do started using them. This naturally didn't suit the railways, so to try to stop it they labelled second-class carriages— 'Second class and servants'. Such was the snobbery of the time, that it worked. Although today the idea of travelling in an open truck may appear extraordinary, it doesn't seem so long ago to me that upstairs in the buses was open to the elements, and that the only protection in the wet weather was a sort of mackintosh cover for the legs. There was no smoking allowed inside and even in the most inclement conditions there would be a cluster of smokers sucking away. And today the government think they'll cure the habit by putting little notices on cigarette packets!

It was while mum was working at Mrs Stafford's, that Queen Victoria died. Mum, I am sorry to say, reports that she was quite unaffected personally. She had never been able to feel any kind of affinity to her or any love for her. But she says, 'I was an exception. Most working-class people wept copious tears and mourned her passing as if she had been a fairy godmother to them, and yet the lot of the poor was the same at the end of her reign as it had been at the beginning. They owed nothing to her that I could see. The other servants went around snivelling for days. I got so wild with them, I said to them, "Come on you might as well peel the onions, it's not going to make any difference to you." '

Mum seems to have got cynical rather young. 'Queen Victoria,' she says, 'very rarely saw, or was allowed to see, how the poor lived. She talked a lot about her beloved subjects, particularly as she grew older, and the older she got the less she saw of them. Absence made her heart grow fonder and it was easy to love in the abstract sitting on a nice comfortable secure throne.' Mum thinks that for the working class Queen Victoria was an outward and visible symbol of God. When you were ignorant and poverty-stricken, you needed something to believe in and the spiritual side of religion was not enough. Also they had precious little to be proud of, so it helped them exist to be able to boast that a third of the world was coloured pink, that Britannia ruled the waves and that no matter how bad things were for them, it was better to be British than anything else. Mum, with her friendships with other servants, has been able to compare the effect of Victoria's death between the aristocracy and the middle classes. The aristocracy she thinks, had anticipated it, were ready for it and were able to accept it, some even gratefully. Her last few years had been a bit of a drag on their lives. She cast a shadow and there were many on the fringe of the Prince of Wales's society who could see gayer, happier things to come, but knew that they would not be wholly acceptable until Victoria was out of the way. The time had come when they had had too much of a good thing. The middle classes, although they aped the manners of the gentry, were less secure. With the Queen on the throne they had had an example of morality, respectability and the kind of family life they held so dear. It had gone on so long they knew no other and they didn't want it to change. Any change was bound to be for the worse and it could threaten their existence. So they tried to preserve the memory of 'our good Queen' as long as they could. They went into mourning and they stayed there. It suited their book. When they talked of 'the Queen' for years after, it wasn't Edward's wife, it was their dear, beloved Victoria. Even when I was in service in the twenties, middle-class morality was dictated by Victoria's example, and we were expected to abide by it. Again today when we talk about 'permissive society' unconsciously, I think, we are comparing it to the Victorian times. For the aristocracy their society has always been permissive; they did as they liked, and hostesses for a weekend party used to plan who slept next to whom with as much care and tact as they did who sat next to whom at the dinner table. Wife swapping was as common then as it is today. During both wars practically everyone was permissive, and what about the flappers of the twenties? Their gear and behaviour was as way out as the hippies of today, despite the way Barbara Cartland may interpret it. It's my opinion she's either got a very short memory, or she went around in blinkers. We keep harping back to Victoria, men do particularly. As far as they are concerned, they never had it so good. As an ardent feminist I agree with that Indian interpretation of her: 'Queen Victoria very fine man!'

The Staffords took Victoria's death stoically, but behaved fashionably. They went into full mourning for a month and then into half mourning for another five months, sort of gradually introducing a little colour into their clothes. The grave demeanour was preserved around the place, but as mum had cause to realise their sorrow didn't affect their appetites. I've noticed this after funerals. The mourners seem to work up a great hunger and thirst. If ever I'm depressed I always seem to eat more. It must be some sort of compensation.

Behaviour patterns were slow to change after Edward came to the throne. Although mum says it was soon after that she and the other maids started using powder. They bought little booklets—

tore off a leaf and rubbed it over their faces to take the shine off. The leaves were supposed to smell of violets, but mum says they didn't smell like any she'd ever picked. Looking back on it and with hindsight, she coins three phrases; that in Victorian times it was private pornography and public prudery, that Victoria caused the flowering of the middle class, but that Edward was no gardener, and that the release from the rigid Victorian rule was like the feeling you get when you took your stays off after being tightly corseted. But again, most of the changes were gradual and generally only affected the attitude and behaviour of the rich. For the poor is was the difference in the music-hall jokes and the style of the popular songs that showed the beginning of a new era.

It's been like trying to get blood out of a stone to get mum to talk about the various boy friends that she must have had around at this time. Perhaps it's her respect for the memory of my father which makes her reluctant to acknowledge their existence. I know they must have been there, because she married quite late for the times, and she has hinted that the reason was that she was having such a good time socially, that she didn't see the point of going steady with one chap. She's not quite sure what made her change her mind. She won't say that she fell in love, that would be showing her feelings and mum's never been one for doing that, or giving any outward signs of affection. As children we had the knowledge of being loved and cared for without any of the demonstrative signs like hugging and kissing. It was never the practice of working-class people to wear their hearts on their sleeves. It was a sign of weakness.

The reason she felt she must have a steady boy friend was that both Kate, the housemaid, and Lucy, the parlourmaid, were courting and she felt she was missing out somewhere. Lucy had, as I've said, been going steady for fifteen years with a policeman. She was now nearly forty. Now under these circumstances I would have thought that any girl, or woman as Lucy was, would have given up any idea of ever getting him under starter's orders, let alone to the post, but according to mum, Lucy was as sure of her wedding day as she had been when they first started to go out. Matrimonially, of course, a policeman was a good prospect;

he'd a steady job with a fair wage and a pension when he retired. Although Lucy wasn't exactly an oil painting, she had
hidden charms; in the savings bank. Over a hundred pounds in
fact, which was a nice bit of money. It would go a long way
towards setting them up in a pub, which was eventually the use
it was put to.

Kate's intended was a dustman and of course of no comparable
social status, as she was frequently made to realise by Lucy.
Being a dustman had certain advantages though, as they were
able to collect bits of furniture which people discarded and were
put out among the dust-bins. All right, they may have been a
motley collection, but after a bit of carpentry they were not to be
sneered at, except, according to mum, by Lucy who would say,
'What period are you furnishing your parlour in, early Georgian
or late Mrs Smith.' When this wedding day was getting near, this
dustman burst in with the news that he'd acquired a double bed
and mattress for two shillings, from one of the houses he ser-
viced. They were both cock-a-hoop about it. It was a different
story after their wedding; instead of enjoying a night of married
bliss, they were both kept too busy scratching and wriggling. The
mattress was infested with bed bugs.

Having made up her mind to go steady, mum had of course to
find the right man. Here, she says, fate took a hand. She was
clearing up the dinner things one evening, when one of her
younger brothers came down with a message from home. He
brought with him a friend of his, a boy called Harry. And he was
a boy; he was two years younger than mum. Anyway they sat
around while mum got them something to eat and then they
began chatting together. Suddenly mum says, it came to her that
this Harry was the man for her. 'Sort of love at first sight,' I
suggested. 'I don't know about that,' said mum; she always shies
away at the mention of love. 'I just decided that he was the one I
was going to marry,' as though that wrapped it up. It did of
course. As I was later to find out, when mum made up her mind
about something, it happened.

It wasn't all that easy because although Harry liked her, he
didn't want a steady girl friend. He was very much enjoying life

as a bachelor and was a member of a gang that, when they had money, would frequent the pubs of Brighton and Hove and, when they hadn't, would stand around on street corners or roam around making themselves a nuisance to all and sundry. So in order to be in Harry's company, mum had to become part of this gang and trail around on her evening off with five or six of them. 'You were a sort of gangster's moll,' I suggested. 'You read too many of those American magazines,' mum retorted. 'It wasn't a bit like that. I used to sit drinking with them in pubs or go with them to a music-hall. At first it wasn't easy because the rest of his mates didn't like having a woman around and showed it. I remember one night when they nearly got your dad away from me. They decided to go to a fair in Rottingdean and all rushed out of the pub to catch a bus. Naturally in my heavy skirts I couldn't keep up with them, and realising that I wouldn't make it, I gave up the chase and started limping along. I saw your dad getting on the bus with the others, but then he changed his mind, jumped off and we spent the evening together. After that I was gradually able to wean him away from the gang and keep him more to myself.' It's on small events like that that history is made!

Harry really wasn't a very eligible young man. Apart from his wild nature he also had the disadvantage of being a painter and decorator, which was at the time a very insecure sort of job. It was largely seasonal so that there were many periods of unemployment; and there was no dole. Because when he had money he liked spending it, mum found she had to finance him when he wasn't working, and although Mrs Stafford didn't know it, many of his meals came from her larder. Mum's family were very much against him, but since her mother was still a bit strange, her opinion didn't go for much, and her father, never knowing when he might have to call on mum's help again, was very careful not to cross her. Strangely enough Harry's mother was all for it. I say strangely because Harry was her only son, there were two daughters, and mothers have a way of hanging on to only sons. She had been widowed when Harry was seventeen. Her husband had a heart attack and dropped down dead in the street. 'What a wonderful way to go,' her friends and neighbours said, but then they hadn't been left a widow with three children. Luckily she had a lodger at the time, 'Old Lou', and after a decent interval he stepped into Harry's father's shoes. Mum thinks the reason Harry's mother welcomed their relationship was that she was worried about her son's wilful ways and, having been in service herself, saw in mum a calming down sort of influence, someone to keep him on the straight and narrow. Old Lou's opinion wasn't asked or given but mum always had a great affection for him. He worked in the local brewery as a cooper, and of course there were a quantity of barrels to be made in those days, since bottled beer was practically unknown. Bottles were another invention that were eventually to put a lot of men out of work and also half do away with a highly skilled trade. Kegs have of course completed the job, and the taste of good beer has been lost. I liked Old Lou. I remember, as a child, thinking at first that he smelt rather nasty. It was, of course, the smell of malt and sour beer. All men who worked in breweries were the same. It got into their skin and no amount of washing or bathing could get rid of it; not that Old Lou used much water. I soon got used to his aroma, in fact I grew to like it, which probably accounts for my early taste for beer.

Mum's courtship lasted five years, and during all this time she continued to work at Mrs Stafford's. I have tried to find out what she and dad did together, what they talked about, how their relationship ripened and how eventually they were able to fix the day and why. To start with, the term 'walking out together' is a literal one. They did walk, wet or fine. They scoured the countryside for miles around. They also drank together in a pub where it was warm and cosy and where Harry's prowess at darts often earned them an extra beer. Their main amusement was the music-hall, and mum is still a mine of information on the comedians of the time, and any of the old tunes she hears on the radio sends her croaking into song. Occasionally, as a special treat, they would take a day trip to London, shop gazing and ending with a visit to the theatre. Mum says they found plenty to talk about and when they didn't they just enjoyed each other's company.

I suppose that's what the expression 'keeping company' really meant—that you found each other's presences all sufficient. You didn't want or need anyone else around. Nor did you have to announce your engagement, wear a ring, give a party or print it in the newspapers. It was a thing between two people, you didn't flaunt it, you didn't talk about it, it was a relationship that you established between you, others didn't matter. Today it has to be seen and heard about to be believed.

Already though mum was establishing her authority over Harry. I noticed when I talked about this time to her that she refers to it as, 'When I was courting your father.' After hearing this a few times I became a bit exasperated. 'But I thought it was the man who did the courting.' 'Not with us it wasn't,' said mum. She is still shocked at the way girls rush into marriage nowadays. 'How can they possibly know whether they'll want to spend their lives together.' Mum maintains that in her day they did know.

She's also against allowing a man to go too far, as of course most mothers are even today, though it seems to me they quickly have to accept the inevitable. She cites the case of an aunt of hers who was courting for nearly twenty years. She was about forty when she walked up the aisle. 'But,' says mum, 'she was able to wear white with a clear conscience. Arthur her intended had never laid a finger on her, he'd been content with the occasional kiss.' She says this as though they were a couple that all should emulate. I would have thought that such a marriage was doomed from the start. Either on their wedding night they wouldn't have known how to begin or else they would have passed out in the frenzy and excitement of it all. When I talk to mum about the frustration, she doesn't seem to understand. 'We didn't think about that side until after marriage,' she said. She calls it 'that side', she never uses the word sex. 'But surely you, Kate and Lucy used to talk about what would happen in the bedroom, when you were together in the kitchen,' I said. 'Never. We used to discuss the kind of houses we hoped to have, and how we would look after our husbands' creature comforts.' 'All right,' I countered, 'then if you were all so virtuous, never feeling temptation, so never having to resist it, how was it that you were always telling my sister Pat and me to be careful with our young men. Telling us the awful things that might befall us. It seems to me the male species have turned into ravenous animals since your day.' 'Ah,' said mum, 'I knew all about the dangers by the time you and Pat were at that age. Your father explained it to me.' There are times when it's best to give up with mum!

Another aspect of courting then which I find interesting was that once you were going steady together there was a rule of absolute fidelity, you never looked at or talked with another young man with interest, and to be seen out with one, even over a cup of tea in a tea-shop, was like being caught in adultery. The social consequences for the girl were just as bad. She was dubbed as flighty and unreliable and her chances of marriage were severely diminished. Just one fall from grace was as bad for the reputation as 'sleeping around' is today.

I've said that courtship was a thing between two people. There were two exceptions to this. The occasions that put the seal on it and made it official; when the young man took his intended home to meet his family and have tea, and vice versa. The Spanish Inquisition and its tortures had nothing on these. This habit spilled over into my time, so I knew what it could be like. It happened as always on a Sunday, and Sunday teas, like Sunday dinner-times, were a big event in working-class lives. There was always something like winkles, whelks or jellied eels. The table was set with knives and forks and the vinegar, salt and pepper were in the middle. You had brown bread spread with margarine and cut quite thinly; none of the doorsteps that you got during the week. Then there were the cakes, treacle tarts, scones and sponge sandwiches; everything you could think of, and woe betide the young man or young woman who couldn't wade through every item, murmuring comments of approbation with every mouthful. 'I could see,' the mother would say, 'that he/she doesn't like the way we live. It's evident to me at any rate, that he/she looked down on us, though what cause he/she should have to do so I really don't know.' There the seeds of doubt could be sown. Then for some there were the younger children to contend with. At first they would probably just gaze at you, having been instructed on pain of death to behave themselves and keep quiet. It was pretty awful to suffer a number of pairs of eyes following your every movement, but then when their good intentions and their behaviour disintegrated there would be giggling and whispering to fight against. Love, they thought, was soppy and they went out of their way to show you what they thought. You had to steel your nerves and try and answer the penetrating questions that were put to you by the parents, particularly by mothers. No matter how innocently they were framed, you knew what was behind them. Did you know how to cook? Could you sew and mend clothes? Could you knit and darn socks? Would you be attentive to his very need? Or if you were a man. What do you do? Does it bring in money? Will you be able to provide for a wife and a family? There was rarely any thought about what he/she could do for you and never any consideration about your love life together, which after all must be the basis for any happy marriage.

Then, of course, there were the inquests afterwards. You'd say to your mum, with bated breath, 'What did you think of him?' 'Well,' mum would say, 'I think he has certain very good qualities but...' and it was that 'but' that mattered, not just what followed it. It was that air of her knowing that he wasn't what he ought to be, that worried you, even influenced you. Then dad might say, 'His job's all right but there's not a lot of future in...' So if you weren't careful you were thrown into a state of insecurity. Parents in those days were an influence. Brothers and sisters you could cope with. You expected them to be derogatory, but they were more careful if they were approaching the age of courting themselves. Those Sunday teas, according to both mum and me, were devastating. On the other hand they did help to make assurance doubly sure.

Now, of course, I come to what may appear to some the disillusioning crunch about mum. To me, knowing her and knowing myself, it isn't really. This is the kind of discovery that after a lifetime of being moralised at and dictated to, comes as a sort of relief. Some bigoted children might have been appalled. I wasn't. It proved to me that mum was human. It brought her closer to me than she'd ever been. I only wished I had known it earlier. You see despite all her homilies about virtue being its own reward, despite her going on as to how she had no sexual feelings until she was married, I eventually stumbled on the fact that the date of her wedding and the date of the birth of her first child weren't compatible with the ideas of respectability in those days. It was when she moved recently from her old people's flat to stay with my sister and I was packing up her papers that I found out. I compared her marriage certificate with a birth certificate.

When I told her of my suspicions she said, 'Footling nonsense. You don't want to believe everything you read. Bert was a premature baby and that's all there is to it. The reason I got married when I did was that I'd watched Kate and Lucy with their long courtships and I'd reckoned that romance faded as the years passed. Also your dad seemed to be pretty used to having his meals that Mrs Stafford was providing, in the kitchen. But the main reason if you must know was that I had my fortune told, and the day we got married was the one the cards said would turn out to be the best. There's no truth in what you're saying at all. Still,' she said huffily, 'you think what you like. You know how happy your dad and I were together. That's all that really counts. Reasons are unnecessary.'

Chapter Seven

Mum's wedding took place at the Congregational Church in Ventnor Villas, Hove. She didn't wear white, not just because of anything that had happened but because they really couldn't afford it. She had to have something that would come in useful afterwards and no matter what you do to a white dress, dyeing it and remodelling it, it always shrieks wedding dress to you afterwards. She did wear a white hat, but no veil. As she said, dad had been looking at her face for five years, it seemed pointless to cover it up on the day that he was taking it on for life. The reception was held at her mother-in-law's house. This was unusual, even for working-class people who, though they often shared the expenses, generally observed the etiquette of holding it at the bride's parents' place. It was generally felt although mum's mother's health had improved to some extent, the excitement and work might have proved too much for her and she could have gone berserk; then the whole wedding day would have been ruined. Not only did Harry's mum provide the place, she also paid for everything. Mum had cooked the wedding cake some time before at the Staffords', with madam's consent, mum says, and with her giving the ingredients, except for the half bottle of brandy that was in it, which in any case was cook's perks.

Mum now feels a bit guilty about her attitude towards her mother-in-law. She took so much that she did and was for granted. Since she's been one herself she realises what a difficult role it is to play. Mum says she was always made welcome from the start, but she put it down to the fact that her mother-in-law looked on her as a sort of animal trainer; someone who had taken over her wild son and trained him into a civilised being. So she felt she'd got the whip-hand and could dictate what should happen and what her mother-in-law should do for her. In my experience, if mum thinks she's got the whip-hand she jolly well has, and she wields it. I think it was in this period that mum developed the strong over-riding personality that she's had ever since I can remember, and which grows more dominating with age. God knows what she'll be like when she's a hundred I tell her!

The wedding reception went very well. It was a small affair, mostly relatives. Her mother kept her senses, nobody got drunk and although Old Lou was a bit merry he didn't come out with any dirty stories or bad language which he was inclined to do when he'd had a few.

Harry was out of work and had been out for a week or two, so there was no question of going away for a honeymoon. They just couldn't afford it. Nor could they afford a place of their own. They moved in with mum's mother and father. They were given the large front bedroom and the use of the kitchen, for five shillings a week. By now both mum's younger brothers had moved out and her parents were living alone. There's a strange sort of irony about this situation when you consider mum's earlier relationship with them. I said this to mum, and added that surely she could have got a room in another house, for the same price. 'I know that,' she said, 'but apart from the fact that I sensed somehow that there would probably be another crisis at home, and that someone would have to be at hand to save them from the workhouse and the asylum, I knew that the place was clean, and you couldn't guarantee that with other houses.' By clean she meant that there were no bugs, fleas or mice. Most similar houses were infested with one or all of these things, and although people had learnt to live with them, mum hadn't; she's always had a horror of dirt and all that goes with it.

They furnished this room. The floor was covered with cheap

89

linoleum, which cost a shilling a yard. 'It was so thin,' mum says, 'we were able to cut it with scissors.' One of her brothers made her a table and some rough chairs. They bought a bed for ten shillings, but after Kate's experiences, she had the mattress fumigated. She was also able to persuade her mother-in-law to part with a few things. Mrs Stafford had given her five pounds as a wedding present, so that bought towels and bed linen. 'We were as comfortable as we could hope to be under our circumstances,' she says. 'I'd never been so happy in my life.'

Nor did mum miss going away on a honeymoon. 'I always thought they were a waste of money,' she says, and I agree with her and not just because of the money. You're suddenly thrown in strange surroundings into the company of a man. I know you've got to live with him for the rest of your life, but it's in the context of his working life. He isn't going to be with you all the time, so to be continually in his company for twenty-four hours a day and with the added burden of physical contact through sex, with the fears and embarrassments as well as the excitements it brings, can be a great shock. It takes a lot of standing up to if you're a woman and a virgin as I was. It can start up a lot of difficulties that might have been delayed until you were better able to cope with them. Dodgy things honeymoons, or they were in mum's days and my days. Now of course, people have often had two or three before their married, apart from indulging in every-day sex.

Mum and dad did have a week together after their marriage, but a lot of this was spent doing things around the place and making their home comfortable. Mum hired a bicycle and they went out for rides together. The first day they took a picnic and, according to mum, were settling down in a delightful spot in the country when, as she says, 'A wasp stung me on the rear.' 'How could it's sting get through all those layers of clothes that you wore then?' I asked innocently. 'It was a big wasp,' was the answer. I've always thought that on any excursion into the country you should always travel with a blue-bag, the application of which may not be a doctor's remedy, but which I've always found effective; I told mum this. 'Even if I'd had one, I couldn't have applied it to my behind in front of your father,' mum replied. 'Well, you'd had one night together.' 'Yes, but this was in daylight, it would have been shocking.' Ah, those rigid rules of sex and nudity, anything pertaining to them had to be done in the dark and with the blinds down.

The next day, despite the wasp sting, they went off cycling again. Again mum was in trouble. To avoid running into a child she swerved and hit a lamp-post. The front wheel of the bike was buckled beyond repair. Poor dad had the job of taking it back to the shop, thus establishing what was to be the normal pattern of his life. He was always to be the one to face the music and to apologise. Mum remained blameless and aloof. It could never be her fault if anything went wrong.

The week after the wedding dad started work and mum had five weeks of married bliss. Then came a long period of unemployment. Things got so desperate that mum wrote to Mrs Stafford asking whether she, or any other lady she knew, needed someone to do the charring. I asked her if writing this letter wasn't a big blow to her pride; after all as cook she had been head of the household. 'Poverty and Pride make poor bedfellows,' mum replied. By return, Mrs Stafford wrote back to say that she had a job which she thought would be more suitable. They had a country cottage in Crowborough in Surrey, about twenty-five miles from Hove, and they needed someone to look after it and to cook for them whenever they wanted to stay there. There was no mention of dad going there with her, though Mrs Stafford said he could stay with her over the weekends. Well, after only having been married such a short time, mum didn't want to be separated from dad, but they had no option; they couldn't live on love, not for any length of time anyway, so she accepted. Dad used to cycle over on Saturdays and back Sunday evenings. It was a steep climb getting there, but an easy ride back. Except for one night; he'd left it rather late, it was very dark and was blowing a gale. Mum says she had a presentiment that there'd be trouble as she said goodbye to him. She often says that she has this gift of second sight and she lays more claim to it the older she gets. I tell her it's being wise after the event. Anyway off dad set. He didn't get very far. It was said that he ran into a tree that had fallen across the road, but dad always swore that someone had stretched a rope across the road. Whatever it was, he was knocked unconscious and wasn't found until next morning. He was seen by some farm labourers, who carried him to the nearest house, which happened to be a pub. As mum said, after she'd got over the shock, 'The only time he was in a pub and wasn't able to enjoy himself!' Apart from a large lump on his head and a piece of one ear missing, he wasn't badly hurt, but it was enough for mum, she gave up caretaking at Crowborough and got a job charring at a house in Portslade, for a Mr and Mrs Hardacre. She worked there from nine to twelve. As she says disappointedly, too late for breakfast and too early for dinner. Free meals were the thing you looked for when you were on the bread line. It was mum's first experience of working for lower-middle-class people. She didn't like it. Mr Hardacre was a solicitor's clerk, who had worked with the same firm, in the same job, for thirty-seven years. His lack of success had embittered Mrs Hardacre, and she was forever running her husband down, not to mum of course, but to her friends and neighbours. She remembers her with her Pomeranian dog in her arms, saying, 'Even this poor dumb animal thinks more of me than my husband.' Since the dog was constantly being fed on titbits and kept up a continual yapping, mum couldn't see where the 'poor dumb animal' bit applied. Mum talks with scorn about Mrs Hardacre. 'The trouble was, mum, that having worked for the gentry and the upper classes, you felt a bit snobbish towards her,' I said. Mum disagreed, 'No, it's not that. The point is that the people I'd worked for in service were accustomed to having servants and knew instinctively how to treat them. They didn't have to show their superiority. They knew they were your superiors in every way so they didn't treat you as inferior. Nor did they have to be on their guard in case they let themselves down in front of you, and, as in the case of Mrs Benson when she took an axe to the Colonel's door, they didn't give a damn if they did, they knew they could get away with it. The trouble with me and Mrs Hardacre was that I knew she was my inferior: I'd got a loving husband, a child on the way,

I was better educated, I read more and understood more, and as a result of my time in service I had better taste and better manners. She was a dried up, embittered, ignorant thing.' Whether mum is once again being wise after the event or whether those were her true feelings at the time, doesn't matter. Her attitude shows again the way education was beginning to affect the attitudes of workers towards employers. There was no longer this blind acceptance. Money didn't matter and was not used as a standard by the working class. When you start querying the behaviour of your employers your respect for them decreases, you find you don't work whole-heartedly, you start to take the mickey out of them, you wonder what you're doing there and for your own self respect you look for another job. This wasn't and couldn't happen in most areas, but it was beginning to in domestic work where you lived in such proximity to your employers that you got to know them as well as they knew themselves, and sometimes better. Hence, I suppose, the saying, 'An officer is seldom a hero to his batman.'

Mum was just thinking about looking for work elsewhere when Mr Hardacre had an accident and got himself killed ignominiously. He was walking across the road in Brighton when he was knocked down by a postman's tricycle. They were sort of big square things with a large red box, two wheels in front and one behind. They were, I think, mainly used for delivering parcels. Apparently Mr Hardacre had a weak heart, and being hit by this finished him off. There were, of course, a lot of crocodile tears from Mrs Hardacre but these quickly dried when she saw the will and discovered that he'd left what little he had elsewhere and that the house was mortgaged to the hilt. 'Just like him,' mum heard her say to her sister. 'He couldn't do any good while he was in the world and he couldn't leave it in a proper way.' Strong words in those days when superstition had it that you should never speak ill of the dead.

Since mum was now well on in her pregnancy, she didn't bother to look for another job. Both she and dad were looking forward to having a baby, despite the lack of money. She'd booked a doctor. His charge was a guinea, paid well in advance.

Having booked him that was that, you didn't see him again until the baby was arriving. There was no such thing as monthly visits. It was the same with the very poor when they were ill. They didn't call a doctor until they could see their patient was nearly dying, and by then they often decided it was too late so it wasn't worth it. It wasn't being stony-hearted; it was being stony-broke. Mum, of course, had been busy making baby clothes and a lot of things were needed in those days. Babies wore so much it was a wonder they could breathe. Long dresses for three months, then these were shortened. Even boys wore dresses for at least a year. Size was considered of most importance in babies, the fatter they were the more prizes they won at baby shows.

Mum decided to give birth on a Sunday, which was a great mistake. The doctor had arranged to play golf. He stalked up and down, being rude to dad and cursing mum under his breath. When it came to four o'clock his patience ran out and he decided to remove it with forceps and without an anaesthetic. What butchers some doctors were in those days. I had my first baby removed by forceps, but I was given an anaesthetic and that was painful and awful enough. Dad, of course, was worried sick. He was rushing around boiling up kettles and cleaning up. Nowadays husbands talk about sharing in the births of their children by being with their wives. In those days working-class husbands had to; not by choice but by necessity. They were in and out of the bedroom all the time helping the doctor.

Although they were delighted to have a son, mum says that without a doubt he was the most miserable baby ever, he howled all night and most part of the day as well. She could now well understand how people could leave their unwanted babies outside a police station, particularly if they had a grudge against the police. Unfortunately mum couldn't feed the baby herself or indeed any of her other children. This was a disadvantage for any working-class woman as it meant stopping whatever she was doing to prepare the baby's meal, as well as coaxing it to feed. She reckons now that she didn't find the right food for him and that he was constantly suffering from the wind. Apparently I, who was the next to arrive, was a model of behaviour, so either she learnt from my brother or I've just been of a jolly disposition all my life. Needless to say, I didn't have to have forceps, I was only too anxious to get into the world. She didn't even have a doctor, only a midwife, who for fifteen shillings attended the birth and visited every morning for a week. Cheap and cheerful, that's me.

Fortunately dad was in work at this time. Despite the lack of sleep, for the first time in his life he was consistently punctual. He was only too glad to get out of the house for a bit of peace. I asked mum, since dad's job was so unreliable, why didn't he try and get a more regular type of work. Apparently at that time it wasn't possible to change at all. As a boy of fourteen, dad was apprenticed to his uncle, who was a painter and decorator, and over the years he learnt his trade. When he started it seemed a good idea, there was a lot of work about, it was better paid than labouring; eventually, to some degree, you became your own boss, and dad liked the work and was good at it. The disadvantage was that the trade became overcrowded, so employers kept cutting their prices, work became scarcer and less profitable, but by then it was too late for dad to change. There were no government training schemes and he couldn't afford to start at the bottom and learn a new trade. He just had to make the best of a bad job for most part of his life. In those days, once you'd made your bed you had to lie on it. The poor were the poor. I suppose the best illustration of what a painter's life was like is contained in the book *The Ragged Trousered Philanthropists*, one of the first great social and socialistic documents.

After the birth of the baby the family loyalty thing worked once again, this time to mum's benefit. Her elder brother who'd got a good job as an engineer on board ship sent her clothes, food parcels and sometimes money. Mum by now realised that she had another cause to be grateful to this brother. He had been about eight years old when mum had been taken to stay with her mother, and had known all the time that she was illegitimate, yet never once had he taunted her with it or told her other brothers or her school-mates. It was a big secret for him to have kept, particularly because she knew she had often irritated and teased him when she was young.

The pattern of her life now became clear to her: it was to be struggling to keep herself and dad and a family (because she knew she would certainly have more children) when he was out of work. She knew she would have to be the main fighter and she toughened herself for the battle.

As if life wasn't hard enough, another crisis hit her. Her father lost his job at the waterworks. Although he was sacked, it wasn't entirely his fault. Some two years back he had developed an ulcer on one of his legs, why he never did find out. I suppose today some men do, but now they can be cured with antibiotics. Then the doctor advised using poultices and gave him a jar of boracic ointment. These didn't do any good. The ulcer got bigger and bigger until it eventually got down to the bone. He kept going to the doctor, who finally shrugged his shoulders at it and told him he'd have to learn to live with it. During this time, of course, the pain had increased and he became desperate. He was constantly scanning the papers and sending away for the wonderful panaceas that he saw advertised. Sometimes he would pay as much as a guinea, but none of them did any good, and his anger at being cheated added to the pain in his leg and made him more morose than ever. He had never suffered his fellow workers kindly. Now he became so irritable that no one would work with him; the boss was told this and he was out. There was of course no pension, no compensation of any kind and no sympathy for his ailment. Always a bitter man, he now took against society completely. Never would he work with or for other men again. Without a job he could no longer afford the rent, so one evening he announced that he'd got two rooms for his wife and himself and that mum, dad and the baby would now have to fend for themselves. They had a week to find another place. Since at that time dad wasn't working, for the moment mum thought there was nothing for them but the workhouse. She quickly put the idea out of her mind and set about trying to find a solution to the problem. Once again Mrs Stafford was her guardian angel. She and her husband were going abroad for six weeks, and they asked if mum and dad would be resident caretakers while they were away. Not only did they get a roof over their heads, they were given thirty shillings a week and free heating and lighting.

Meantime mum's father and mother had moved to two rooms in Fishergate, Portslade, a town which adjoins Hove on the coast. Her father had saved a bit of money, and while he had studied the newspapers in search of a cure for his ulcer, he'd come across a number of advertisements for making money by working at home. One of these was for a machine that knitted socks, a sort of forerunner to the modern knitting machines. 'Everyone needs socks,' he said, and decided to invest in one of these. Mum says it was a peculiar looking affair shaped like a saucer with needles sticking up all around the brim. In theory you fitted the wool over the needles, worked a lever up and down and in no time at all a sock appeared. In practice the needles which should have stayed put, jumped around and the wool got tangled and knotted, or else one needle would refuse to function so that you got a ladder down the sock. Mum's father stuck at it, and as she says, him being a trained engineer, if anybody could have got the thing to go, he would. Finally the lever came away in his hand so he flung the thing out of the window in his fury and went into one of his black morose moods for days.

When he recovered from this, he decided to become a market-gardener. Despite his painful leg, he worked hard at this and the results were most spectacular; but apparently it doesn't matter how good the harvest is, you've got to know how and where to sell it. He didn't, and since if you've got something to sell you have to ingratiate yourself with the potential buyer, and since he could never ingratiate himself with anybody, this venture ended in complete disaster and a lot of rotten vegetables.

He then saw another advertisement for a kit for making rag rugs, which were all the rage at that time, so he decided that he and his wife would work at this sort of cottage industry. Between them they made some beauties, but again they had to be sold, and since everyone was making their own, this proved impossible. I must say 'it's an ill wind' because mum came in for a few of these rugs. I can remember them around the place up to the time I went into service.

The last of his get-rich-quick schemes came about as a result of his ulcerated leg. Having been written off by his doctor, he'd started experimenting with various ointments himself, sort of mixing them up together and hoping that in this way he might find a cure. Sure enough one day he did, and his leg began to heal quite quickly. So here at last was the God-given opportunity not only to make money, but to do good while making it. He bought lots of little pots, had labels printed, and advertised his miraculous cure in the papers. Unfortunately what was sauce for the goose wasn't sauce for the gander, and it was only a short time before he started getting irate letters from sufferers who were still suffering, demanding their money back. What didn't help matters was that his own ulcer had broken out again and was soon as bad as it had ever been despite frequent applications of this, his own amazing cure. The climax came when the police visited him and accused him of fraud. Apparently even mum's father's arrogance collapsed in the presence of the law. He was asked to explain, how he with no medical knowledge, had thought that this ointment could be a cure for ulcers. 'It cured mine,' he said. 'Let's have a look.' Well he was caught literally with his trousers down. There it was, sore and nasty, in front of their eyes. He wasn't prosecuted. Mum reckons that the police were content with a good laugh at his expense. But it was the end of his attempts at home industry.

By now all his savings had been dissipated; mum's father was broke, and there would have been nothing left but the workhouse for them if mum's elder brother hadn't helped them out. Once again comes this example of the family spirit of the time. 'Supposing he couldn't have offered to give help,' I asked mum, 'would the other brothers have contributed?' 'They couldn't have afforded to,' she says. 'They weren't a great deal better off than your dad and I were, the workhouse would have been the only answer.' 'Did your brother give the money because of the slur of having parents in the workhouse?' 'No,' mum says. 'It was the accepted thing with the poor. After all if a man only earned eighteen shillings or a pound a week and had a wife and five or six children, farthings became important. The budget just couldn't stand any additional strain. It was bad luck if your mum and dad had to go there, but nobody thought the worse of you because of it. It was accepted that you would have done your duty by them if you could have. Again there was none of this stupid business that there is today of keeping up with the Joneses. There weren't any Joneses. People were either poor, middle-class or rich, there wasn't any in between, and they lived in communities according to their status, so the poor lived with the poor and everyone in the street was in the same boat. There was no competition.'

When the Staffords came back, dad was in work again and since they'd saved a bit of money they decided to launch out. They rented a whole house with the idea of letting off two rooms and thus defraying a large part of the rent. Mum decided that she would be the best landlady that tenants had ever had. Along came a charming couple, with a young child, a Mr and Mrs Carlisle. For two weeks everything went well, but week by week another child was introduced into the household until eventually there were five. What the Carlisles had realised, of course, was that no one would let two rooms to a couple with five children. Mrs Carlisle said at first that they were looking after them for friends, who had gone away, but the friends never seemed to come back and claim them, and two children looked too much like their parents for mum to be deceived. Eventually chaos reigned. By that time I was born and mum was expecting another, there were seven kids and four adults. Life became impossible with the noise and the overcrowding in the kitchen and the lavatory. Mum gave the Carlisles a week's notice. They didn't budge. She then thought about calling in the police to evict them, but she didn't know how to go about it. In any case nobody called in the police in those days if they could possibly help it. In the end dad and she gave a week's notice to the person who owned the house, they moved out and left the problem behind them.

They now took just two rooms for themselves. They didn't strike the ideal landlady. According to mum she was one of those fuss-pots who wanted everything to be just right all the time. Of course I know now that she tends to see the situation just from her own point of view. There's no six of one and half a dozen of the other about her. Apparently this landlady had a fetish about cleanliness, which I should have thought brought her near to mum's heart. It didn't. They were expected to wipe their feet every time they came in and dad, when he got back from work, had to remove his boots outside the back-door and carry them upstairs. Children were to be seen but not heard. You name it, mum had to see that it was done. I doubt it. I think by now mum was getting so tough that if things didn't go her way she was the one that was being hard done by. She was the heroine. She won't admit to there being faults on both sides. But when I explore a bit, I find that while she was in this particular place, dad's employer, who had promised dad that he was going to make him a partner, went bankrupt. When this happened he asked dad to store his stock of paint and wallpaper, as well as his brushes, planks and ladders, so that the official receivers wouldn't get hold of them. Mum says that both their rooms were lined with pots and rolls and outside the back yard was cluttered with ladders and things. Well, it's not surprising that the landlady took against them. Somehow they managed to placate her; mum thinks it's because dad, being out of work, offered to decorate the outside of the house in lieu of rent, and made a very good job of it, using of course his previous employer's materials.

It was at this time that mum didn't know whether to put a penny in the gas meter for lighting or to buy a pennyworth of oil to cook by. She couldn't go out to work herself as she was expecting her third child any time. In fact he arrived on Christmas Day, financially the worst time possible because no painters and decorators were in business then. I've often taxed mum on why, when she knew dad's work was irregular and there was no dole when he wasn't working, she continued to have children. Her answer is simple. It was the only pleasure they had and it cost nothing. It was the only thing that made them equal with all society, with kings, princes and governors; and the working class had more energy and therefore more appetite than those other three so it gave them a feeling of power. Birth control was largely unknown. Mum and dad did know about it but couldn't afford it and wouldn't have used it even if they could. In the act of sex the man was dominant. His pleasure came first and he wasn't going to have it minimised by what he thought of as a sort of motor tyre, and since mum was in love with dad then and always, and since (and I'm certain this was really at the back of it) she enjoyed herself as much as he did, she wasn't going to be wilful and deny him or herself. Then of course the infant mortality rate was very high at the time. Not, I think, that parents consciously thought of this, but losses, while not anticipated, were reckoned on. I remember when Albert, my husband, and I were first married and living in London, the woman in the rooms below us had the welfare woman around complaining about the way she was bringing up her children. She called in her mother who went for the welfare woman: 'I've had twelve children of my own and I've taught my daughter how to bring up hers, you can't tell her or me what we ought to do.' What she omitted to say of course was that only three of them were still alive.

On the other hand according to mum, when women got pregnant they accepted it as being, as it were, all in the day's work. They didn't moan about it, nor did they drink gin or have hot baths, in the hope of getting rid of it, and abortions were almost unknown; except the back-street abortions for unmarried girls. Then when the baby came they welcomed it and brought it up as best they could. A child just had to take its chance. Life of course was much more of a community thing then. People were in and out of each other's houses, helping with the confinements, doing the washing and looking after the other children while the mother was still in bed, helping out with the baby's clothes and requirements. I remember when I was having my first child, being presented with a list of essential things. Well, it would have run into pounds to have got them and we couldn't afford it. I showed it to mum. 'Stuff and nonsense,' she said. 'You can tear that up and listen to me,' and she told me what I'd have to buy, which was precious little, and what I could borrow from friends and neighbours. 'Having a baby's not a major operation,' she said so convincingly, I believed her at the time. I wasn't so sure a few months later during my confinement.

Today it would seem that the time between the pregnancy test and the birth is inadequate for the thousand and one things that have to be done. Entire rooms are redecorated and refurnished, libraries of books on pre-natal care, baby care, and child psychology are bought and studied, there's a wardrobe full of clothes awaiting the little darling and a zoo of stuffed animal toys to add to his confusion when he gets into the world, as well as a series of conveyances to get him around the place from a carry-cot to a car seat. There's a hell of a lot of outward show but I don't believe there's a ha'porth more love. There is too the other side of the coin, those couples who go about complaining that they didn't want a child, that it will adversely affect their way of life and that they don't know how they're possibly going to be able to afford it. If they'd lived in mum's time, they wouldn't have dared to voice those kind of sentiments. They'd have been ostracised and their lives wouldn't have been worth living.

Mum's third baby coinciding with a family financial depression, meant that mum had to take advantage of a scheme known as 'The Bag'. Through this scheme you could hire a large cotton bag which contained sheets, pillow cases, towels, all the things you needed to see you through the confinement. Afterwards you washed and ironed everything and it was passed on to the next mother-to-be in the locality. It was useful if you were broke, but mum didn't like using it because as it was hired more often the things got worn, and as some people weren't too fussy over the washing, the colour of some of them turned from white to a nasty grey. I've spoken to people about this 'Bag'. They are amazed and appalled when they realise that sheets and pillow cases and such things weren't in everyday use. They find it hard to believe that even blankets were a rarity in working-class homes. When we were children we had pillows with just their tick covering, and we lay on a mattress covered with a thin patched piece of blanket; we had one blanket to pull over us and the bed was then covered in old coats. Sociologically poverty can be very interesting, experiencing it is just plain foul.

Although I was only four when this baby was born, I remember very well the Christmas day he arrived because I was taken by dad to stay with his parents. I particularly loved 'Old Lou'. He was the antithesis of my other grandfather. He was like a character out of Dickens and always completely uninhibited at any holiday time or time of rejoicing. He made a great fuss of me, throwing me up in the air and catching me, letting me sit on his knee and jogging me up and down; he even let me work the pride and joy of his heart, his phonograph. It had a huge horn and played roller-type records. We all thought it a wonderful invention, even though the needle would keep slipping off the roller. We sang little duets together. He was the only person who ever enjoyed hearing me sing. Mum says that's because he was deaf. I think she was a bit jealous of the attention he gave me.

The years leading up to the First World War were, mum says, the worse she'd known financially and nothing has ever been quite as bad since. Despite this she still maintains they were happy ones and from what I can remember of it, our home life was. Mum never nagged at dad over his inability to get regular work, she knew he did the best he could, so the chill of poverty was offset by the warmth of family love. Two more babies arrived and there was the odd miscarriage. These extra mouths to feed hit mum harder than any of us. She starved herself so that none of us went hungry. Her staple diet was a cube of Oxo in hot water with a lump of dripping added. Fortunately too, the soup kitchens had opened in Hove, and as I've said in *Below Stairs* it was my job to go along at midday with an old china wash-stand jug, which was covered in pink roses. I used to suffer agonies of embarrassment. It was bad enough to have to queue up for charity soup, but all the others had white enamel jugs to collect it in. I was therefore a complete pariah. We were seldom short of bread because every other morning my elder brother and I got up at six o'clock and went round to the baker's with an old pillow case and queued up for the stale bread. It wasn't all that stale, only yesterday's, and we'd get enough for the family for two days, for only a few pence. Nevertheless mum still had to deprive herself, and proof that she did so is in the fact that when my sister, Pat, was born, she weighed only four and a half pounds, yet mum had had the full nine months' pregnancy. It's also interesting that Pat has had better teeth than any of us. When she was about twenty, the dentist remarked on them and said, 'Your mother must have drunk a lot of milk before you were born.' 'No she didn't,' said Pat. 'She drank Oxo.' This set him back on his heels because he'd never heard of Oxo as being a source of calcium.

So the pattern of life continued for mum, having babies and trying to feed a growing family on an uncertain wage packet. She could see no end to it and no change. I'd like to be able to report that she'd observed the war clouds gathering on the horizon, but she hadn't and neither had her friends and neighbours who were in similar conditions. She and dad both read the papers, but the places and the people that sparked it off were too remote for them to believe in. In any case the only kind of war that they could remember had been the Boer War, and this they thought of in terms of a series of skirmishes. It hadn't affected their way of life. It wasn't a battle for survival. It was something that went on between soldiers, it was something they went away to do and it didn't concern the civilian population except to bring out the occasional bit of patriotic fervour and the feeling of 'Thank God I'm British'. In any case the newspapers seemed to think the affair would blow over, and in those days people believed almost everything they read in print. Mum's war at that time was a personal one, waged in Hove. A battle of survival for herself and her family.

Chapter Eight

Although the actual declaration of war was a shock and therefore an occasion that merited a visit to the pub and a few extra beers, the flurry soon died down, particularly as everyone said it would be over by Christmas as though that day had some special significance war-wise. In its train it brought a rumour that was to excite our street and many of those around us and to send housewives cleaning, polishing and scouring their houses and rearranging their furniture. It was that soldiers were to be billeted on the town. I couldn't see how this could affect us as we had only three rooms and a kitchen. Mum had other ideas, particularly when she heard that the billeting rate was nineteen and six a soldier; this included accommodation, providing and cooking their food and doing their laundry, but it still sounded a lot, indeed it was a lot at the time. We children were to sleep in the sitting-room, the baby was to move in on mum and dad, two double beds would go into what had been our bedroom and hey presto, there would be enough room for four soldiers. All mum had to do was to convince the billeting officer. She did. While this meant a certain amount of nocturnal discomfort for us children, we had to sleep in a three-foot six-inch bed, two one end and two the other, it had its compensations and we suffered in silence, at any rate in front of mum.

Our home, which had never been exactly spacious, was now overcrowded to say the least, but there was a bustle and excitement such as we'd not known before. Our soldiers consisted of two Englishmen, both countrymen, big with large hands and red faces, a bit slow-witted but very amiable; a Welshman and a Scotsman. The Scotsman was our favourite, he was a gentleman. By that I mean he spoke in a deep cultivated voice, and did things like standing when mum came into the room, opening the door for her, and knowing how to use a knife and fork; he was also a remittance man. Some years before, he'd been sent to Canada by his family to get him out of the way and out of trouble. The war, however, was an excuse for him to come back and still continue to collect his two pounds remittance money. I fell in love with him on sight and so it's my belief did mum, but she'll never admit it. 'He made me feel a million dollars,' is as far as she will allow herself to go. Unfortunately the Welshman fancied mum and her obvious preference for Jock, the Scotsman, started a series of quarrels which eventually ended in a brawl and nineteen and six or no nineteen and six, the Welshman had to go. He was not replaced and Jock had a double bed to himself.

It may seem ridiculous, but my feelings for this Jock were so strong that I became jealous of mum and unconsciously I think we used to vie for his affection. I tried all ways of making him notice me. I'd run errands for him, polish his buttons, I even used to clean his boots. And I'd be consumed with jealousy when I saw mum waiting on him hand and foot, and him following her into the kitchen when dad wasn't there and helping her with the cooking or the washing up. Hearing them chatting and laughing together used to be a torture for me. I think that young as I was I knew that he wasn't doing it for an extra portion of pudding. I can't be sure to what extent the relationship between them ripened, I only know that mum bloomed as I'd never seen her before, so did all the other women in the street, so that may prove nothing. Dad I remember as being uneasy and disconsolate for the first time. Mum didn't realise my feelings for Jock, and she won't accept them even today. She reckons that seven and a half is too young to have feelings of affection for anyone except your relations. Parents can show a lack of understanding even when you're sixty-four and they're ninety-one! I remember how I used to resist it when one of the country soldiers would try and get me to sit on his knee in case Jock should think that my affection for him was waning. I'd take sweets and comics from the others but I didn't repay them with any special attentions.

For me those billeting days were my first glimpse of paradise, but there had to be an ending and this didn't just come when the soldiers were posted abroad. Jock had an appetite for drink and above all for whisky, the wine of his country. I never saw him the worse for it although mum says there were occasions when she knew he'd had one too many, even though he always behaved like a gentleman. 'It's not surprising,' mum says, 'because many mornings before breakfast I'd have to go over to the pub and bring back two shillings' worth of his "golden liquid" as he used to call it, and every evening he would spend in some pub or other.' It was this habit which was to bring about his fall from grace and to cause the collapse of my ivory tower. He fell for the bar-maid in our local. Now that in itself was no sin, but he decided to marry her. In those days you didn't marry barmaids, not even in the working class. I suppose some people must have, but in our street and in our society it was unheard of. Well, of course, it caused quite a furore both in our house and in the neighbour-hood. Mum tried every trick she knew to dissuade him, but he was resolute. She even had words with the barmaid and such expressions as 'Jezebel' and 'scheming woman' were bandied about. His marriage didn't do mum much good in the eyes of the neighbours who had come to look on their soldiers as part of the family. One of mum's family had disgraced himself and part of the blame they felt must be hers.

Monday mornings had become a great occasion in our street. This was the day when the sergeant came round to pay the billet-ing money. What a contrast they were to the Mondays before the soldiers came. Then wives could be seen taking their husband's best suit and shoes to the pawn shop to raise a little money until pay day, or I would be sent to do the shopping and would have to gather my parcels in my arms, so that when it came to paying

I would say, 'That's all right mum will settle at the end of the week,' as I rushed out of the shop. Now I could go anywhere as bold as brass, pay with real money and get some change. There was a sergeant for each side of our street. The one who called on us was young, handsome and amorous. He got so frisky that mum found it best to go to the door with the baby in her arms, as a sort of protection. Even that didn't put him off, he tried every ruse to get into the house like wanting to show mum photographs of his wife and family. Mum wasn't having any. She'd got her hands full enough, apart from the baby. From what she said though, the sergeant did pretty well down our street with the husbands out at work, the children at school and the soldiers on parade. Like mum I didn't care for him either. I think it was because one day when I answered the door, he beamed at me and said, 'I've got a little girl at home just like you,' and showed me a photo of a skinny rat-faced child.

After they'd been with us about three months the soldiers disappeared as quickly as they'd arrived. They were sent to Shoreham, where the Army had built a new camp. You'd have thought our street had been smitten with the plague it seemed so quiet and deserted. The housewives went around with long faces and, according to mum and dad, the pub was like a morgue. Within a few months quite a few of the women were carrying a lot more weight and it wasn't just because they'd been eating well. Eventually the birth rate took a noticeable leap and mum says many a husband anxiously scanned the face of his new-born baby to see if it bore any resemblance to him. She particularly remembers poor Mrs Ferring who lived a few doors away. She was called poor because she'd been trying to have a baby for years without any success and she'd been up and down the street asking advice from the more fecund. She went to old Ma Shepherd who'd had fourteen. 'Get yourself another man,' had been the somewhat brutal reply: 'Or you can borrow my bugger if you like.' Poor Mrs Ferring didn't need to, because as a result of the soldiers moving in, in the fullness of time she gave birth to twins. Well of course this took a bit of explaining. Mr Ferring seemed quite satisfied with the doctor's diagnosis that it was the excitement of the presence of other men in her house that had made her suddenly fertile. Mum thinks the doctor's interpretation might have had some sound medical reasoning behind it, but others weren't so charitable.

For the kids, the departure of the soldiers affected our stomachs. Meals went back to normal, and normal wasn't very much. Prior to the war, we hadn't had meat, cakes and jam regularly, so not having had them we didn't miss them. Now, of couse, we were loud in our complaints and felt we were hard done by and undernourished. It was a bad time for mum, she didn't sing around the house as she had been doing. She didn't have to work so hard of course, but work doesn't seem like work if you're happy doing it. One bright spot was that as more men were called up, there was more work for dad, not so much in the painting and decorating line but by now he was a fairly proficient odd job man.

Mum's attitude towards the progress of the war was a selfish one. The historic events that she read about in the papers interested her but were interpreted by her as, 'How is this going to affect me and mine.' She has never been a patriotic woman and at that time she felt she owed nothing to a country that had presented her with such a hard struggle for existence. As for world issues like starvation in India or China, these were as remote to her as the moon. In any case she had been nearly starving herself so she was in the same boat as them; she didn't know about nor understand comparative conditions. At first mum thought things in Britain had improved with the war. The trouble with Ireland subsided, the trades unions were quiet, the suffragettes had turned their energies against Germany instead of the government and the civilian population were told to carry on with their usual work. In dad's case there was the proviso, 'If he could find it.'

After Belgium was invaded mum was cynical, 'All this fuss about a country that two weeks before only one in fifty of the working class knew existed. I'm afraid I couldn't shed any tears over it, though to listen to some of the people in our street it was as if someone had debauched their wives.' A lot of men were filled with patriotic feelings and took the king's shilling, but a few weeks later when they came back on leave, their hatred for the Germans had changed to a more vitriolic loathing of their sergeants, and they were concerned about their own mental condition at the time they had joined up.

Charlie Harris was the exception in our street, mum says. Charlie was about thirty, handsome but unmarried. He didn't see the point of marriage, he could get all the girls and all the fun he wanted without any of the responsibilities. He was a proper tearaway, popular with young people of either sex but the bane of any mother with a daughter of marriageable age. The stories of his sexual prowess were legion. In his case I was able to verify what mum said because Charlie only lived two doors away and had a sister of my age, and she used to tell me about Charlie's girl friends and their goings on. He fascinated me in a sort of way and I liked him because he noticed me and few people bothered with children of my age. Perhaps he believed in cultivating young girls, thinking ahead about ten years of the fruits to come. Charlie didn't confine his activities to single women. I remember being woken one night by tremendous banging on a door down the street. I went to the window, and it was a Mr Burgess beating with his fists on Charlie's house, and shouting, 'Where's my Nancy? Where's my Nancy? Come on out or I'll smash the door in.' Well, there was a lot of verbal toing and froing and eventually Mr Burgess left. The next morning I mentioned the incident to mum; 'But who was this Nancy he was after?' I said. 'Mr Burgess hasn't got a daughter called Nancy.' 'You mind your own business and get off to school,' mum snapped, which was silly of her really because it only made me more inquisitive. My investigations proved that Nancy was Mr Burgess's wife, so I eyed Charlie with even more awe then.

Anyway getting back to mum's story: 'When Charlie announced at the beginning of the war that he had enlisted, there was a great excitement in the street. He was considered a hero by some, and even the mums who'd been fearful for their daughters started knitting socks and Balaclava helmets as a sort of thanksgiving farewell offering. Charlie came back on his first leave with a stripe on his arm, no chips on his shoulder about the way he'd been treated, and proceeded to have a sexual field day for the week.

'Eventually he was posted to France; no one felt any sympathy for the French girls, they were a loose lot anyway, and the mums relaxed. It wasn't more than three months though before Charlie was back, on crutches and minus a leg. Once again he was the local hero. The mums at first were a bit put out, but they reasoned he couldn't get up to his old tricks with only one limb. They were wrong. He may not have been so athletic on his one leg, but he made up for it in other respects.'

Charlie's popularity didn't affect recruiting because people quickly realised that he was going to find work hard to come by in the future and his pension wasn't enough to finance his way of life. Dad, you will have gathered, didn't rush to volunteer. Mum defends this by saying, 'Why should he have? He was a married man with five children. He felt his first duty was to them. Very few working-class people were imbued with this love of King and Country. As far as they could see their King and Country had done nothing for them.' I can see her point of view. If you've had an easy, comfortable life you warm towards the country that's given it to you and you are prepared to do something in return. There were of course those that, although they had been hardly treated, enlisted. They were either saints or fools, depending which way you looked at it. There is, I think, a final reason why dad didn't join early. If he had he'd have never have got to France. Mum would have killed him first.

When dad did finally go for his medical, he was graded C.3, and sent straight back home. Mum at the time was elated, she didn't think what the eventual consequences might be. The reason given for his grading was that he had a weak chest and that was because of his job. There was at that time something in the paint, lead I think, which if it was constantly inhaled, affected the lungs.

Mum has told me that when she and dad went to the pub he couldn't swallow the first bit of his drink, he'd have to sip it a few times. When he'd drunk about half a pint, he was all right. However, mum's elation was short lived: chest or no chest dad's country needed him, and a couple of months later in 1916 he was called up. Dad didn't mind very much. He'd got fed up looking at those posters: one of Kitchener saying that his King and Country needed him, and the other of a German assaulting a woman, with the caption underneath of, 'This could be your wife.' I'd seen them too, but I reckoned it would be a strong-minded German that would try anything on with our mum! Her reaction to dad getting his call-up was highly aggressive and not very complimentary to dad. 'Stupid fools obviously don't know what they're doing. The army can't be all that hard up.' She meant because of his chest, of course. She then sat down and wrote a letter to the War Office, telling them what she thought. Mum was always one for action. Needless to say she didn't get a reply. My elder brother and I kept telling dad how we would protect mum. Protect her! It was others that needed protection from her. The family allowance was as near starvation as the government could risk. As children even we knew this and made promises of doing odd jobs and collecting and selling horse manure, in order to help. As things turned out it was back to the old routine for me, telling lies to shopkeepers, the tally man, the milkman, the butcher, the baker and above all, the rent man. I played on their heart strings with my wide eyes and white face. I perfected a pathetic act. The rent collector was the most difficult to deal with. Even today I have nightmares, with him shouting and raving and threatening to turn us out into the street.

When dad eventually left home I missed him more than any of the others did. I think I would have found life easier to bear if mum had gone, and I believe she would have contributed more to the war effort. I loved mum, but since she and I were so much involved in the struggle for survival, there was no place for senti-ment. That I reserved for dad.

Dad only did eight weeks' training in this country. He then had a short leave and was posted to France. I could tell from mum's attitude that she was very upset about his going there. She was quiet about the place and I suspect a bit weepy, not that we ever saw her cry. However she realised she could not be like that for long. She knew there were to be long hard times ahead and she'd got to have the strength to meet them. Also dad's letters started to arrive, both he and mum wrote regularly, and they were reassuring in a way, since he was a long way behind the lines and it was unlikely he would be sent to the trenches. I say in a way reassuring because mum now started worrying that dad might be mixing with French women, all of whom, mum says, according to working-class thinking at the time, were no better than they should be. After all the French were a loose living lot, otherwise they wouldn't have all those brothels; and legalised by the government too. Mum reckons that that song 'Mademoiselle from Armentiers' didn't help to keep the *Entente* very *Cordiale*. The major household problem around this time was fuel. Coal was severely rationed and although we cooked by gas our rooms were heated by open fires. The only way to get a bit over the odds was to say that you needed it for cooking purposes. I was sent up to the Town Hall to do the necessary perjuring, by signing a form to this effect. I had also to lie and say that mum couldn't come because she was ill. Then I had to take an old pram and the form down to the coal depot and queue there for half a hundredweight at a time. I also had to watch the kind of coal they gave me. Because they thought I was young and wouldn't notice, they tried palming off the coal dust on me. After the first time they didn't because mum came back with me and the coal dust, turned it out in front of them, gave them a piece of her mind and made them reload with the proper stuff. Even though we'd got this extra permit, we couldn't always afford the money, so mum used any wood she could find in the house, shelves, old chairs, even some of the banisters, and we children went beachcombing along Hove sea-front for any bits we could find.

Mum says that the only relaxation she had at this time was a weekly visit to the music-hall with her sister-in-law. They walked there and back, and sat in the gods. One night, when she and her sister-in-law had parted ways, a soldier tried to pick mum up and he offered her a shilling for her services. Mum says she hit him, which I don't doubt, she also waxed indignant that she should be taken for one of those kind of women. I don't think it was righteous indignation at all and I've since told her so. 'You were furious because he thought you only were worth a bob, mum.' It was just as well I was going out of the door at the time.

In order to supplement the army allowances, mum went out charring in the mornings. She tried to get work with Mrs Stafford, but this time she was unlucky. Mrs Stafford had had to cut down her staff as a result of the war, and her own circumstances had been reduced and she couldn't afford extra help even when she needed it. Mum got a satisfactory place though at the house of the man who owned the laundry. It was the same laundry that I was later to start regular work at. Whether it was the thought of dad among the French girls and a desire to be able to compete with them when he got his leave, or whether they were giving her trouble I don't know but mum decided to have her teeth seen to and a visit to the dentist showed that she needed to have them all pulled out and a complete set of false teeth fitted. This, of course, cost money, a lot of money, two pounds ten in fact. To get this meant she would have to work afternoons and evenings as well. Mum was determined, so she got a job as a school cleaner. She visited the dentist once a week and though he caused her considerable pain, she suffered in silence.

She really did look something when she got her new teeth. She went around all the neighbours showing them off and perpetually grinning like the Cheshire Cat. 'That dentist has made a new woman of me,' she said. It was more than mum did for him. She'd one more visit to make to him, just to make sure that they really fitted. When she went round she was told he'd died the day before. When I said how sorry I was, she said, 'Oh it's all right, I don't think they needed any adjusting.'

Dad never got leave from France. One night, after he'd been away for about six months, there was a heavy banging on the front door; it was just about midnight and we were all in bed. It woke me up. Mum and I crept nervously down, and then there was dad's voice calling to us. Mum suddenly turned and dashed upstairs. 'Coming, Harry,' she said as she went. I didn't realise till later that she'd gone to fetch her false teeth from the side of her bed. When she opened the door she threw herself into his arms and I think it was the first and only time I ever saw her cry. It didn't worry me because I knew they were tears of happiness and joy. In any case I was the same. Well of course by now the whole family was roused. It was a time of great rejoicing. 'Why didn't you tell us you were coming home on leave?' mum said eventually. 'I'm not,' said dad, 'I'm in this country to stay.' Apparently his health hadn't been too good out there and the army had decided that he was more of a liability than a help to winning the war. They weren't going to discharge him but he'd been posted to Newhaven, about eight miles along the coast from Hove, for home duties. In the meantime he'd got a week's leave. Mum was cock-a-hoop. We children, after the first excitement of seeing him had died down, started to look around. Our eyes fell on his kitbag and we wondered what kind of exotic luxuries he'd brought back from France. We were to be disappointed, he hadn't been able to get anything for mum except, as she later remarked, a pile of dirty clothes. All he'd brought with him was a large collection of French lice. All his things had to be boiled to get rid of them. Despite the lice, mum had a wonderful week and with dad being stationed so nearby the parting wasn't so sorrowful. We children, I think, felt a bit let down. We expected dad to come home with all sorts of adventurous stories about France and the war. He didn't mention either. He felt, I suppose, that he hadn't done much. Mum has told me since that he got fed up listening to others who were on leave, talking in the pub about how they were winning the war. He maintained that most of the real heroes weren't alive to tell their story and those that were never shot their mouths off about it.

It wasn't long after dad went to report for duty at Newhaven that he found himself what soldiers call a cushy billet. The adjutant of the barracks there, a Captain Clarke, had a large farm outside the town, in a village called Piddinghoe. When he found out that dad had been a painter and decorator, and was also a good odd job man, he put him to work on his farm. He made the excuse that dad needed outside employment because of his health, and that by doing farm work he was contributing to the war effort. It was a big fiddle really, because dad was immediately put on to painting his house inside and out and the labour costs, and indeed some of the cost of the paint and materials, were down to His Majesty's government. Not that dad worried about it. In any case, apart from making his life easier when he himself wanted to arrange a few perks, it made his position practically invulnerable. For some weeks dad was billeted on the farm and used to come home when he got free time on Sundays. This arrangement didn't suit mum, particularly when she heard that there were a number of women employed on the farm, sort of equivalent to the Land Army girls of the Second World War. She decided to let our rooms in Hove and take a furnished cottage in Piddinghoe. We were all very excited about moving into the country. It sounded marvellous, and mum told us stories of the wonderful times she'd had in Shoreham. It's all fine in the past or the abstract, isn't it, but in fact it was a disaster. Mum hated it almost from the start and we children very soon caught mum's mood. The cottage we went to was cold and damp. All the water had to be fetched from a communal pump and therefore hoarded because the journey was long and muddy. Washing is not something children ever enjoy, even in a kitchen sink, but washing outside because there is no sink, is sheer torture. We didn't have an inside loo in Hove, but there was a water closet near the backdoor. To have to traipse down to the end of the garden, where there were two earth privies shared by four cottages, was by comparison barbaric. Even our neighbours found the smell revolting, either that or they had no finer feelings, because they used them with the doors open. Then there were the paraffin oil lamps, all inadequate and a chore after gas light. Cooking on an open fire was another thing mum wasn't used to. I think, though, mum and we children could have put up with all these things, almost have learned to accept them, if it hadn't been for the chronic boredom of the place. Nothing ever happened there. We reminded mum of what she'd told us about Shoreham when she'd decided to move to Piddinghoe. 'It was nothing like this,' she said, and then she thought a bit. 'Perhaps it was but what you've never had you don't miss. I must have been a proper little cabbage when I left Shoreham and we shall all of us become the same if we stay here much longer.' Mum missed our street most of all, the wit and malice and the sharpening of her mind on the people around her. There was a village pub, but no women used it and mum felt out of place even being there with dad. 'The other men used to sit staring at me. I'd wonder what they were thinking, probably nothing, country people didn't seem to go in for thinking a lot, but it made me feel uncomfortable.' There was one shop, a combined village post office and general store. It was kept by a Mrs Penfold, who'd had eighteen children. Rationing was at its height and mum, being a 'foreigner', didn't get any of the extras that the other women did; these were sold under the counter. 'With Mrs Penfold and her eighteen children that wasn't the only thing that went on under the counter, mum remarked somewhat acidly. Mum had further cause to be unfriendly with the Penfolds, but that came later. For her weekly shopping she had to walk two miles to Newhaven and two miles back, down a dirty, dusty road, which added further to her dislike of the place.

We children used to go to the village school. After the one at Hove it seemed antiquated. There were only two classes in one large room, which was separated down the middle by folding wooded shutters, but since you could hear in the one what was going on in the other, it was often very difficult to concentrate. The country children didn't seem as far advanced as we were. They, I think, automatically disliked us or at any rate they were suspicious and wary of us. Because of their attitude towards us we thought them stupid, and if we got angry with them called them country bumpkins. This wasn't true. They knew so much that we didn't, the names of the trees, birds, flowers, and they got pleasure from the land. The fact that we knew the names of cars, the streets of Brighton and Hove, the buildings, the shops, the theatres and the numbers of buses that took you to these places was of no interest to them. They'd learnt how to live without these things and were probably better for it, but children don't like being different and don't really care for any permanent change. They also believe that whatever mum says is right and so, like her, we were resentful of the life we were leading.

During the six months we were in Piddinghoe, dad didn't really enjoy his home life. To mum that cottage couldn't be a home and although there was never a row between them I sensed that feelings were not what they had been. It wasn't for many years that I was to learn that, apart from the surroundings, there was someone who had intruded on their lives and who, although never causing a split between them, did test mum's loyalties then and later. The event that made mum decide that she couldn't stay any longer was seemingly a trivial one. A Mr and Mrs Morris, who lived in our street at Hove, arrived one Saturday morning with Mr Morris's old mum. They were a lively family, and their main pleasure was cycling around the Sussex country-side. Because his mum had passed the age when she could pedal, Mr Morris had bought a second-hand bath-chair, one of the wicker sort which ordinarily was pushed from the back and steered by a handle attached to the small wheel in front. Being a bit of a mechanic, he'd made some sort of an arrangement by which this bath-chair could be fastened to the back of his bike, and he could pedal her along behind him. Very ingenious it was, though it did look a bit comic and occasioned many laughs and cat calls from people, particularly children. The old lady, how-ever, took it all very seriously. She looked so gracious sitting there in a long black dress with her pure white tresses, part covered by her bonnet and part waving in the breeze, a rug over her knees and her gloved hands folded in her lap. Yet the set up was some-how incongruous. It became even more so if she heard people mocking at her. Her features would distort and she'd shout worse invective than had ever been hurled at her. Sometimes her gloved hands would unfold and she'd throw stones at her mockers or make a gesture. Winston Churchill had nothing on old Ma Morris. The young Mrs Morris was also a bit of a sport; winter and summer she'd bicycle down to the sea-front first thing in the morning and have what she called her early-morning dip. She hadn't any children and people used to say it was because of this habit of hers. She also took in visitors during the summer and because her house was on a corner and on a clear day you could see the sea from her top window, she called it 'Sea View'.

After the three Morrises had spent the day with us and gossiped with her about the goings on in our street, mum got a fit of the nostalgias, so when dad came in that evening she said, 'Harry, I've always told you I would go through fire and water for you, but I won't rot and ferment. I've become a blooming cabbage. I'd nothing to say to the Morrises except to belly-ache about the life here. The children are the same, so we're leaving and going back home.' Well of course we kids were all delighted. Once mum had spoken we knew there would be no argument. She set out the next day, gave the tenants of our rooms a week's notice and within a short time we were back in our own world again. I reminded mum of this 'fire and water' bit recently, and asked her how she could equate what she said to dad with it. 'Well,' she said, 'if you go through fire and water you're considered by everyone to be a heroine, whereas if you rot away in the country nobody notices and I've never been one to suffer unnoticed or in silence.'

Poor dad, the onus was now back on him. Once again on Sundays he had to make the journey home to visit us. It now became clear why he was glad in more ways than one that Captain Clarke, his adjutant, had made this rather underhand arrangement for dad to work on his farm. Every Sunday morning he would arrive with a laden haversack on his back. When he opened it up it would be full of margarine, sugar, tins of bully beef, joints of meat, things that at any time would have gladdened a housewife's heart, but which in war time were manna from heaven. They were, of course, dad's pickings from the stores Captain Clarke was filching from the army. What was right for an officer was right for his men according to dad's reasoning. 'But why didn't you get us this when we were in Piddinghoe?' asked mum. 'Too small a place, people would have talked,' dad replied. 'But what if you get seen bringing it here?' 'No chance, I walk across the Downs and when I get into Hove no one's likely to bother.' Mum didn't worry any more, indeed she got bolder as the weeks went by and started exchanging things at our street shop.

During the time we'd been away things had changed quite a bit in our street. There was a different sort of atmosphere. People were tired and sick to death of the war, morale was low, there was a feeling of peace at any price. Then as the war took a turn for the better, mum got a telegram. Telegrams were things that, delivered to a working-class home, only meant one thing, bad news. The mere sight of that red envelope filled anyone with foreboding. This was no exception. It was to say that dad was seriously ill in the Military Hospital at Newhaven, and would mum go at once. I was sent down the street to borrow the fare from Mrs Morris, and mum rushed off to catch the train. She was gone for what seemed an eternity. I remember one of our neighbours coming in to give us children a bowl of soup, but I couldn't eat mine, I just sat there crying and thinking of dad dying. Eventually mum got back and told us that he'd got the Spanish flu. It was a horrible thing, a sort of plague that swept this country and Europe. To many it seemed like God's retribution for the terrible war that we'd been fighting. It had a strange sort of irony, for there were many men who had served almost continuously in the trenches from 1914 to 1918 and got away with it, only to be killed by this epidemic when the war was nearly over. I'd heard about it before, because a barber near our street was shaving Isaac Darke, a bookie's runner, one morning when he fell down dead, with the razor in his hand. 'He might have cut my bloody throat,' Izzy was reported to have said unfeelingly. I remember laughing at the time, but now it had struck so close to me, I was worried sick. For the next three weeks mum went every day to the hospital. It was a wretched journey for her, but slowly dad recovered. The doctors and nurses seemed to think it some sort of miracle that he did because of his weak chest. I am sure that the miracle was mum. She pumped her energy into dad by just holding his hand. She willed him to live. It's an ill wind that blows nobody any good; as a result of this Spanish flu, dad was discharged from the army earlier than he otherwise would have been. He was invalided out on a full pension of thirty shillings a week, which was just as well because mum had almost bankrupted us paying the fares to and from Newhaven; he was also able to get a job before the labour market was flooded with ex-servicemen.

Chapter Nine

When the war finally ended, and I say finally because for us it had ended when dad came back home, everyone went mad with joy. I was at school when the news of the armistice was announced and I remember we all sang 'God Save the King' and one or two other patriotic songs, gave three hearty cheers and were then sent home for the day. I'd never seen the streets so crowded, everybody it appeared wanted to be with somebody else. They had all left their houses to talk and to rejoice. Mum, dad and we children all did the same. We wandered happily up to Queen's Road, the road leading from Brighton station. It was blocked with a solid mass of gay, laughing people, linking arms, dancing, throwing streamers and just being joyous. People were swearing life-long friendships with each other; class didn't exist, there was a general feeling of abandon; of release from worry and care. It wasn't just that we'd won the war, it was the knowledge that war and its suffering was all over. It was thanksgiving in its true sense. No one at the time realised that bullets were a clean death. That survival could and would eventually lead to a mental anguish that was to be worse than the fears they had experienced in the trenches. Mum, I know, was sceptical. She'd had her happiness when dad was discharged. I think she saw the armistice for what it was likely to be worth to the working classes. She was forever on at dad to dig himself into his job, to make himself indispensable. Dad was a sentimentalist. He thought that war had changed human nature for the better. He believed that the politicians really would work for a land fit for heroes to live in. In any case if they didn't, they would be replaced by men who had fought in the war and would insist on a decent deal for their comrades in arms. He didn't anticipate that the country would change overnight, but he did eventually expect a kind of Utopia where the working man would have a decent job, a decent home and would be happy and contented. It was what soldiers had talked about, dreamed about and fought about and died for. He didn't see how the country could break faith with them. Then of course he saw it happen. The demobbed men came back to find there were no jobs for them. They stood around in groups on street corners waiting for someone to do something about them. Nobody did. Then came the street musicians, the match-sellers, the beggars, some who had lost a leg or an arm, the regular band of door to door salesmen, and the ex-servicemen's marches, to draw people's attention to their plight. I suppose there were those who didn't know what was happening to them. It was all too obvious in our street. At first people were shocked and indignant but far from the changes in human nature that dad had foreseen, it was the same old story; they soon got fed up with ex-servicemen, tired of the hang-dog look of them, and bored listening to the tales of what they'd done for their country, and how quickly their country had forgotten them. It was like someone telling you about their incurable complaint. You feel for them at the beginning but when you've listened to the same story for a few weeks, you've had enough; you don't want to hear any more. People didn't want to know about the war when it was over, almost they wanted to pretend it had never happened. Mum sums it up today by saying, 'Everything went on in the same way as it had before the war, except there were more people out of work. That's what the upper classes wanted and that's what the ruling classes saw they got.' She doesn't say it bitterly, just as a matter of acceptable fact.

My own particular memory of the end of the war was of the wonderful party given for the children in our street. It was decorated with flags and bunting, trestle tables were hired from somewhere and set up in the roadway. They were piled high with the sort of things most of us hadn't seen for years—and some had never seen—sausage rolls, cakes, jellies, blancmanges, fruit salads. There were Christmas crackers and funny hats. It was given by the street for the street. We children were waited on by the parents, except the young mothers with babies who sat with us. I remember this because one or two of them were actually breast feeding their babies at the table. After the meal was over there were sports and games. The whole street was more alive and happy than I'd ever seen it before or since. It seemed as if people were convinced that a new and better land was theirs for the asking and I think we children looked forward to sharing it with them.

The more mum and I have talked over those days and remembered and recalled the people in our street, the luckier I think we were to have lived there. The south has a reputation for being inhospitable, of not being so neighbourly as the north. This was certainly untrue of our street. I think poverty and large families were the bonds that kept us so closely knit. We needed each other much of the time, and people seemed to know instinctively when they were required. There would be help for any emergency; births, sickness and deaths. There were many people in our street who were expert at laying out the dead, and since almost the only insurance anyone took out was for the coffin and funeral expenses, death was an event in the street. A decent burial was something practically everyone could look forward to; and the business of 'paying your last respects to the dead' was the excuse for many a hangover.

Again, there was always someone in the street you could call in if ever anything wanted doing in the house or any repair had to be made. You paid them what you could at the time, and you saw them all right in the end because you knew you would need their help another time. One such was Old Dick Tidy. He was a short thin man. He was younger than mum but everyone called him 'Old Dick'. He'd only got one arm. He'd lost the other when he was working in the laundry, as a young boy; it got caught up in the machinery. The owner told him it was his fault, he should have been more careful, gave him five pounds and the sack. Dick later wasn't all that worried about it for, as he said, it kept him out of the war and probably saved his life. He treated his disability as a challenge and turned his remaining arm to any job which came his way, never giving in until he'd mastered it. Like so many small men he had a big wife, who always seemed to be pregnant. She'd presented him with five daughters and Old Dick excused his wife's perpetual condition by saying he was trying for a son. With the sixth child his attempts proved successful. 'Old Dick Tidy could do more with his one arm that most other men could do with two,' mum reflected ambiguously. He had a succession of jobs as I remember, milkman, furniture remover, coal heaver, all heavy work. He also had his own pony and cart and used to do odd carrying or removal jobs on his own account in the evenings and at weekends. Mum says he was an expert at midnight flits. That was moving people and their belongings when they had run up debts or owed a lot of rent and were expecting the bailiffs in. She also thinks that although he always kept on the windy side of the law, some of the people who used his services didn't, since he often had things to sell which were well under the market price.

Some people on the street were unpredictable. For example there was a middle-aged couple who came to live near Old Dick Tidy. They'd no children and for a long time kept themselves very much to themselves. We thought they considered themselves superior, because he had an office job and went to work wearing a bowler hat and gloves. Meek and mild thing he looked, particularly when he was out shopping with his wife. Then he started going into the pub and after he'd had one or two he bucked up no end and by turning out time he was the life and soul of the party. One night as he was reeling home, he saw a light on in his bedroom, and to the delight of those with him he bawled out, 'It's no use you bloody well going to sleep, you old cow, because I shall need you in a minute.' His sudden popularity must have gone to his head because this street call became a weekly performance.

There was another rather pathetic couple I got to know because they paid me a penny a week to do their shopping for them, by the name of Mr and Mrs Stout. Mrs Stout was always going on about how she'd seen better days. She didn't need to because it was obvious to me from the way she spoke. She had a cultured voice, which was something of a rarity in our street and a thing I envied even as a child. One day as I was taking her shopping list, she started talking to me, and I remember rather rudely saying that Stout was a funny name. 'I wasn't a Stout until I was fifty, before that I was a Castle. Castle was my maiden name,' she said. Well, I almost burst out laughing thinking of her as a maiden of fifty. 'I got married to Mr Stout shortly after my father died. I'd spent most of my life looking after him. Such a kind man, my father. When I said I was going to marry Mr Stout, everyone told me I was making a grave mistake because he did manual work but you see he was such a kind man as well and in that way reminded me of my father. And I was so very lonely.' I think except for the company of Mr Stout, she was very lonely in our street too. People resented her going on about what she had been, and if people in our street didn't like you or what you said they made it plain. I think that's why she got me to do her shopping for her.

Mum says that just after the war was financially one of our easiest times, with dad in work and getting his pension. Even so we weren't all that well off, but with mum always busy with her sewing machine, we older children were kept well dressed, and dad had learned to knit and did it well, so the younger children had whole outfits made for them by him. Nobody seemed surprised about his knitting. It wasn't considered effeminate. Even if it had been, nobody in the street would have been courageous enough to have said it in front of mum. This kind of home industry made certain people think we were better off than we were and since in those days it was the poor who looked after the poorer, we had a few callers scrounging things from us—or sending their children along to do it. One such was Ma Phelps, a great hulk of a woman who looked like a Billingsgate fishwife in her sack apron with a man's cap on her head, and she sounded like one too when she opened her mouth. She'd a gravel pit kind of voice, and every remark she made was laced with invective.

She used to pass our house each morning with a large china jug on her way to the local to collect the beer, with her large red face glowing like a sunset under the flat hat. She had nine children and from time to time one of them would be sent along, usually poor snotty-nosed Violet, to ask for something. 'Mum says have you got a pair of knickers for our Glad? Rosie needs a bit of ribbon for her hair, mum thought you might have a piece. Our Ernie's boots are out on the soles, mum says have you a bit of leather.' Our mum would always get them what they wanted, but would send them away with a flea in their ear. 'Tell your mum to lay off the beer for a week then she might be able to buy you something herself.' They never reported back of course. I know from what the shopkeeper told me to say to mum in our hard times. It wouldn't have paid because you would only have got a hand across your ears for giving the message. Ma Phelps stands out in my memory because it was the only house in the street that mum told us children we mustn't go in. It was because of the livestock, the fleas and the lice. Actually she needn't have worried, none of us would have anyway because of the smell there. Today of course, the welfare would have taken over. Yet I wonder how much more successful they would have been. Ma Phelps didn't ill-treat her children. As a family they lived eleven to three rooms. They were brought up rough. You could say their parents were drop-outs. They gave up trying to cope and took to drink, but somehow their kids were brought up or brought each other up, and I'll bet that most of them became good and useful citizens. Whereas if the state had got hold of them, their parents would have been described as 'socially inadequate' and the children labelled as 'deprived', the family would have been separated and the country would have had some costly problems on its hands. There's a saying, 'Leave well alone.' I think, often, leave things that don't look too well alone and they may get better, disturb them, and you've got a hornets' nest around you. I believe, and so does mum, that that was true about our street; we could meet our own and our neighbours' problems.

With what looked like financial security, mum says she faced the future with equanimity. Our standard of living had gone up because she and dad could now go out for a drink three nights a week instead of one and they could really feel they were making whoopee. Unfortunately for us all the Army had other ideas. Dad had to report every three months for a medical check-up. Each time they found his health had improved and docked a bit off his pension; by the end of eighteen months he'd lost the lot. Well of course mum blew her top. 'Inhuman, incompetent old dodderers', she called them. She wrote to the War Office and, of course, again got no reply. She'd have stormed up to Whitehall but dad finally put his foot down. He reckoned she was making a fool out of him. When dad did get around to speaking his mind, mum always took notice. I think often she would go into battle with the establishment because although she knew she was bound to lose, she enjoyed the struggle while it was on. Also it kept her in training and proved that there was still plenty of fight in her. I think, too, that mum became more belligerent when she was pregnant. I read somewhere that lionesses do and I tell her that's how we children used to look on her. I don't think she minds. Being an eldest daughter I used to think had great disadvantages because mum giving birth every two years threw a great deal of work my way. Indeed when she announced she was pregnant I used to get as indignant as those church workers who used to come visiting down our street, telling the women they ought to get their husbands to show more self-control. However, when I came to have my own children, my early experiences were a great help to me and I didn't have any of the fears and worries that many women seem to get today. I did moan a bit about this new baby coming because I was still looking after her 1919 one, Donald. He was my favourite brother. I don't know why I liked him particularly, because he was the most unattractive child to take out. He looked all right, but when strangers stopped to speak to him, he'd bawl his head off. If they attempted to pick him up, he'd use his head as a battering ram and with his hands he'd try to pull their hair out. For some reason, probably because I did so much for him, he seemed to love me, and I could do anything with him. He insisted on my feeding him and he would go to sleep easily if I put him to bed. Perhaps knowing I wouldn't be able to give Donald so much attention was the reason I resented mum's pregnancy more than usual.

Mum kept up her boy, girl, boy, girl rhythm and in 1921 had a daughter. She was named Elsie, at my dad's insistence. I know it was Shakespeare who wrote, 'What's in a name?' He was wrong. This one caused mum some considerable concern. I've mentioned earlier that while dad was in the Army at Piddinghoe and when we joined him there, mum disliked the woman who kept the village shop. It wasn't just the woman she disliked. She had a daughter of about twenty-six, who worked on the farm with dad. Apparently a friendship developed between him and this girl, whose name was Elsie. It didn't take mum long to find out and she was angry and very jealous. She tackled him about it. As I've said dad was a quiet, gentle man. He assured mum that there was nothing going on between the two of them, but when she demanded that he break off the friendship, he refused. Mum tells me that she just couldn't leave it at that, and for the first time in their lives there was a rift between them. This all added to her dislike of the place, and her intolerance, much of which was visited on us children. Dad wouldn't give in; mum says that she grudgingly accepted defeat, but it was this that finally made her decide to leave Piddinghoe. When dad got discharged from the Army and returned home, mum thought that would see the end of it. It didn't. Every month dad went over to see this Elsie, and his visits continued for many years. It was a bitter pill for mum to have to swallow when he insisted on his child being called by the same name.

Like me, although I knew nothing about it at the time, and indeed didn't until many years after dad's death, mum doesn't believe there was anything more to it than a strong bond of affection, but it still hurts her to think of it. I believe she also knows that, had she been a little more understanding, it wouldn't have assumed the proportions that it did. Easy enough to say that now, but what woman would have been able to control her emotions at the time; certainly not one who was as much in love with her husband as mum was.

Elsie was to be mum's last child. Although in many ways she was pleased about this, she had some misgivings. A woman likes to think that she's still fruitful; also it would appear to the do-gooders that came round the houses in our street, that at last mum had decided to take notice of what they said and was practising self-control. Mum hated these do-gooders, as most people did, but she was never downright rude to them. There was always the danger that one day we might need parish relief and their report would be called for, and if it was adverse it could have weighed against us.

I think what mum most resented was being told that if working-class people didn't drink, their lives would be a lot happier. She reckons they got it the wrong way round. It was because the workers had such hard monotonous, insecure lives that they needed to drink. For ten or sometimes twelve hours a day it was, 'Come here, go there.' 'Yes, sir, no, sir.' 'If you don't want the job there are fifty others who do.' The only way a man could feel a man again was by going into a pub. Here there was no one to say him yea or nay. Even if people took no notice of what he said, he wasn't made to shut up.

It was the same for the women. With so many children around it was a life of monotony and often squalor. No matter how fond you are of kids, you like them all the better for having got away from them for a bit. So the pub and its wares helped to release women from the dull drudgery of life. Drink was for most working-class people a compensation, and, as mum says, the do-gooders didn't realise that without it they might have looked for other means of escape and settled for bloody revolution.

A visit to the pub was also, for mum and dad, an opportunity to get away from the house and be together, and now that there were six children and two adults living in three rooms conditions were somewhat crowded. Many people feel that living on top of each other is the cause of acrimony among families. With us it was the opposite. In a way we were forced to live on amicable terms with one another; there was nowhere to escape to if we had rows. Then again, we had few personal possessions. There was a second-hand lady's bike, which we elder children shared, a tricycle and a scooter for the younger ones, and a patched up teddy bear handed down for the baby. Sleeping arrangements weren't too easy. Mum and dad shared the front room with the two youngest children. The two older boys had the other bedroom. My sister Pat and I came off worst because we slept in the kitchen, she in the cupboard under the stairs and I on a camp bed which had to be got out at night, made up and then put away first thing in the morning. There's one thing, we had plenty of company, because as soon as the light was out, a platoon of mice would emerge and start raiding the kitchen. I used to send them scampering by striking matches, but there was one, he must have been the father of the flock, who refused to budge. He'd sit on the floor looking at me as if to say, 'You're much more frightened of me than I am of you.' Once when I got exasperated by the sleeping arrangements, I asked mum why we couldn't share the other bedroom with our brothers. 'You can't and that's the end of it,' she said. It was, of course, that it wouldn't have been respectable and mum was a great one for respectability, providing she was the one who defined it.

My eldest brother, Bert, was the first of us to go out to work full-time. He left school when he was fourteen. He'd already helped the home finances by doing a paper round and assisting the milkman at weekends. A milkman did three rounds a day then, so this kept Bert very busy. For a time it did anyway. It was his job to push the milk cart, which was a three-wheel affair, two at the back and one in the front. It had a large churn in the middle and smaller ones grouped round it and the measures hung on a rail at the side. From time to time these measures would be stove in at the side. If you remarked on it the milkman would apologise and say he was getting another one soon, but in the meantime he had no compunction about giving you short measure. Some used to water the milk too, according to mum. We children were rather proud of our Bert doing this job and often used to follow him up the street. One day my sister Pat and I were watching him. For a moment my attention was distracted. Then I heard Pat running up the street. I looked round and saw that while I wasn't looking, she'd turned on the tap of one of the churns and the milk was flowing out and running down the gutter. I suppose I should have turned the tap off, but I didn't. I ran after Pat. When we came back there was a crowd of kids pointing at us and saying to the angry milkman that we'd done it. What was funny, though I didn't think so at the time, was that every cat in the neighbourhood had also got the message and was lapping away merrily; at least they'd never had it so good. Bert was given the sack on the spot. He tried to tell the milkman it wasn't his fault, but the fault was in the family and Bert had to go. He didn't speak to either of us for at least a week.

Bert's first real job was with the Home and Colonial Stores. He went there to learn the trade. Learning the trade seemed to mean that for half the time he was on his hands and knees, scrubbing the shop out, and the other half delivering goods as an errand boy. Mum with her customary optimism thought that with Bert working in a grocer's shop she would get fringe benefits like a rasher or two of bacon, packets of marge and sugar. Of course she got nothing. With Bert half the day on the floor and the other half on the streets, he never got his hands near any of the goods. I remember once going round to the shop to get something; I was eating an apple I'd scrounged from somewhere, and I saw Bert scrubbing away looking ever so miserable. I took compassion on him, 'Here, Bert,' I said, 'have a bite of my apple.' He didn't say anything then but oh gawd the expression on his face! Talk about if looks could have killed. He told me later how I'd added to his humiliation. He was right of course, as I was to learn when I went into service.

It was now that I met my first boy friend. It wasn't difficult, he was a cousin of mine. His name was Ted. It was what I suppose today would be called a tenuous relationship. It was very much frowned upon by mum. 'You can't marry your cousin,' she said. Who was thinking about marriage? After all I was only fourteen and I'd only been out with him about three times. 'If you marry him you'll have idiot children,' she went on. It made the whole relationship seem incestuous. Parents, I thought at the time, will kill anything. Honestly they will. All Ted and I did was sit in the pictures holding hands. It was enough for me. I felt as though I was floating on air. I really must have got it badly because since he used to go to church on Sundays I went along too. Before, wild horses wouldn't have dragged me there. I'd long since finished having to go to Sunday School so that mum and dad could go to bed together on a Sunday afternoon. Not that they stopped the habit, but now they gave us money so that they could do it. We used to go to a café on the sea-front, order tea and a couple of buns and then take out the rock cakes that mum had cooked for us, put in a bag and thrust into our hands before shooing us out of the house. Nobody seemed to mind. Nowadays if you take your own sandwiches into a pub, the whole place goes mad. But back to me and Ted. In a strange way I found church interesting. The preacher was quite young and good-looking, and very fervent. None of this 'with it' religion stuff that you get today. He roundly condemned all backsliders and prophesied the flames of hell for us unless we repented. When you left the church you felt somebody, either because you were going to go your own way and stick to sin or because you'd reformed and felt a great penitent.

I don't think it was because of mum's attitude towards our relationship or because of church that I got tired of Ted. We just broke up and within a couple of weeks I couldn't stand the sight of him.

Now it was my turn to start work. I had a series of jobs which I have described in my book, *Below Stairs*. It was when I was at the laundry that my grandfather died. After his get-rich-quick schemes had all failed, he had had to settle for becoming a jobbing gardener. He also had his own allotment and made a bit of money by selling flowers and vegetables. Grandmother's wits didn't improve but they didn't get worse and somehow they were able to make ends meet. Eventually granddad got the old age pension and as time went on his legs got really bad and he couldn't work any more, so mum's elder brother supplemented their income and life just dwindled by. Mum went over to see them both from time to time and we children were sent every other Sunday morning. We didn't look forward to it. It was a harrowing experience for us trying to make conversation. Grandfather would take us up to his allotment and show off his vegetables. I remember in the autumn he'd give us a pumpkin or a marrow to take back to mum. Neither vegetable did she want and she'd give us instructions to dump them on the way home, which we gladly did because they were heavy. It was all rather pathetic really. Eventually, at the age of seventy-eight, grandfather died. When I asked mum what he actually died of she said, 'Old age. He just stopped breathing.' I found this hard to believe. There must have been something else put on his death certificate, but mum was adamant. 'People were allowed to die of old age in those days.'

The question after grandfather's death was who was going to look after mum's mother. Although two of the sons were doing very well and had a room to spare, their wives refused to consider having her. They would have seen her go into the workhouse. Well, with eight people sharing three rooms it seemed that mum couldn't be expected to help, but she did. It was arranged that the two elder boys would sleep in the house opposite and grandmother would have their room. The rent of their room was five shillings a week. Mum made her two brothers pay for this, which they gladly agreed to do. They must have reckoned to have got off lightly. Dad and we children accepted the situation at the time, but I have asked mum since why, in view of the wretched treatment meted out to her in the past, she was able to make this kind of sacrifice. 'The past was the past. No point in brooding on it. Anyway something had to be done and since nobody else was prepared to do it, I had to.' 'But you didn't like doing it, did you?' I asked. 'Of course I didn't, but we can't always do what we like in this world.' That, I think, was the philosophy of many working-class people of the time.

I remember that mum was considered by the street to have done more than her duty because people stopped me and said, 'You've got a very good mum. I hope you children will do the same for her if she ever needs it.' We sort of basked in her temporary glory. Even the parish priest called to see her and told her that she was doing a very Christian act and that she would get her reward in heaven. Mum was a bit gruff over this. She didn't see it as a Christian act, and if there were to be any rewards she'd prefer to see them now and not wait for the off chance in heaven. It was quite an event though, the parson calling. Mum only saw him when her children were baptised, and since she had me done at the age of seven along with my sister, Pat, because I'd been forgotten, she hadn't even been the half a dozen times. I must say I've got on to mum about this baptism. Fancy having to share it with a babe-in-arms. It was a humiliation. The parson didn't hold me in his arms, he wouldn't have been strong enough. I just stood at the steps of the font and had the water splashed on me. It really wasn't good enough; sort of two for the price of one.

When I heard grandmother was coming to stay I remember being a bit frightened. I needn't have been. In most ways she looked and behaved like a typical old lady. She'd never been very tall but she'd sort of shrunk into herself. She was the epitome of Joan in Darby and Joan; all the viciousness had gone out of her.

Mentally, of course, she was strange. She had one or two peculiar traits. Some nights she'd leave her room and go and sit on the stairs in the dark with her apron over her head. It was a waist apron, the kind she always wore, but instead of buttoning it at the back she buttoned it at the front. Then she had a large hat pin with a blue head pinned into the side of her skirt. This was to repel people with. Every now and then she'd snatch it out and impale some invisible enemy. 'Get away with you. Be off,' she'd cry. Every morning, providing the weather was fine, at ten o'clock she'd dress up and leave the house to see the carriage and pair go by. Of course there was no carriage and pair. All her funny habits were harmless. She'd the appetite of a horse and although she ate three big meals a day she was constantly hovering around the kitchen to see what else she could scrounge. Her powers of concentration had gone, so that if you were talking to her she'd suddenly get completely lost and just sit and gawp at you. We children of course weren't very tolerant, so we'd try and avoid speaking to her, but we were never allowed to be rude to her. We were warned about this by mum, before she came. Not, I think, that we would have been. People were allowed to be eccentric in those days. For example, a year or two later when I was in service in London, I used to travel home every month on the Brighton Belle. I used to wander along to the kitchen to chat up the stewards and generally ended up doing the washing up for them. They'd give me a drink for my pains and we'd be a friendly sort of party. Today nobody would think of doing that sort of thing. Life's far too regimented. People are too conscious of their 'image'. There was on old lady in our street who always wore a hectic violet bonnet tied under her chin with a piece of string, and she had three short capes, one over her shoulders, one hanging down over her waist and one covering her bottom. Most extraordinary she looked but we got used to her, almost proud of her in a way.

The poor were more tolerant of human frailty than the well-to-do. When I was in service I never once met an eccentric old relation in the houses I worked in. If they had them, and I'm sure some of them must have had, they wanted them kept out of sight, and so out of mind.

It was not long after grandmother came to stay with us that we were offered a council house. This of course meant that the family could all be together under one roof again, so mum took it, although she was sorry to be leaving the street. I was in service when we moved, and with a proper house I felt able to take friends home to tea occasionally. If the friend was male, it could be awkward. Grandmother would stare at him for a long time in silence. Then in a loud voice she would boom, 'Is this your lover, Margaret?' Of course she didn't mean it in the connotation of the time, but my brothers and sisters would be convulsed with suppressed laughter and the unfortunate boy friend would squirm with embarrassment. Give mum her due, she tried to distract grandmother's attention, but it was as hopeless as trying to divert Niagara Falls. Having as she thought established the relationship between the boy and me, the wily old bird would take over its direction. 'Do you like these short skirts,' she'd say. Then she'd tug at mine as I was sitting there, and she'd then stare at my young man. Then mum would get exasperated and shout at her to leave us alone. It wasn't just done for my benefit because mum was also trying to keep with it and had shortened her own skirts, and bobbed her hair. She was always conscious of her personal appearance. I remember when her first grey hairs began to show, she sent my sister, Pat, to the chemist to get a bottle of Valentine's walnut dye. She wouldn't go herself, of course, because to dye your hair in those days was considered shocking, if not downright immoral. It shows how rare it was because the chemist Pat went to had never heard of it. 'You want the hardware shop, my dear,' he said to Pat. 'Ask for walnut stain, and they'll give it you.' Pat, who didn't know what mum needed it for, followed his advice and arrived back home with a bottle of floor stain. Mum didn't blink an eyelid, she just took it and later went out herself and got her Valentine's. It was a rare occasion, for mum couldn't have been into a shop for years. She always got us to go for her.

Chapter Ten

I was fifteen when I left home and went into domestic service. This was a period in my life which I have described in *Below Stairs*, but the feelings I gave there about leaving home were the superficial ones. There were deeper and more personal reasons for my easy submission to taking on a job which I knew instinctively I was unlikely to enjoy, and thought even at the time that I was temperamentally unsuited for. One Sunday afternoon I was out with my brothers and sisters on one of our weekly tea parties, when I remembered I'd left the money behind to pay for it. I rushed back home, went in quietly, and I heard mum and dad's voices raised in anger. I'd never known them to quarrel before. As I listened I heard my name, and to my horror I realised it was me they were rowing about. The gist of it all was that mum was accusing dad of liking me more than he liked her. That when he came back from work he paid more attention to me than anyone else. She was jealous of me. It was a great shock to me. I got out of the house as quietly and quickly as I could, ran back with the money to pay for the tea, and then went off on my own to try to collect my senses.

My first feelings were of indignation. How dare mum think things like that. It was absolutely untrue. She was just saying it to stop dad liking me. Then I began to feel jealous of her; her power over dad, of the fact that she could talk to him about her inner feelings and I couldn't, of her closeness to him. Then I felt guilty. I did love dad so much. More than mum. Yet when I was younger it had been the other way round. I became conscious of the fact that I had gone out of my way to do things for him to make him like me. That I was thrilled by the way his eyes lit up when I came back home and how he seemed to want to talk to me about the things I'd been doing. He didn't just accept me like mum did, he was interested in what I was doing and what I was thinking. I could sense that there was something in what mum had been saying, but I couldn't see that I'd done anything wrong. What I did know was that whatever it was it must be a big thing because never had I heard such a bitter quarrel between them. Since it was such a big thing, I was frightened that it might destroy what I had come to recognise as the one really precious thing we had, family unity and love. I went home after this heart searching without any idea of what could be done to solve the problem. I think I knew I was the only person who could do something about it and I spent many restless nights wondering how.

When I look back I see that mine was the problem of many eldest daughters in closely knit families, and I don't think it's one that can be avoided by having sex talks; it's too delicate and intangible. Sexual feelings don't just come with puberty. I had them much earlier as I think I've shown by my attraction towards Jock, and the jealousy I felt towards mum over him. Essentially a girl needs a male figure to look up to, to work off certain emotions upon. She doesn't know what she is doing, and I don't think it's going to help if she does, but she has an unconscious awareness of man, of the opposite sex. At first it brings with it a feeling almost of fear because of its strangeness. You wonder if you are different from other girls. This adds a sense of guilt; for me a guilt that I'd changed in my attitude towards my parents; that now I loved my father more than my mother. I didn't realise at the time that it was because he was a man and that eventually the same emotions, with the addition of a conscious sexual motive, would be channelled into what is called the right direction.

Mum was never antagonistic towards me, but I believe now that she didn't want me trespassing on an area which she regarded as exclusively hers. She had a nature which demanded great affection from her man. This she got in full measure and running over from dad, but in her opinion there must be nothing of it going to other people. Dad must not be allowed to become too intimately attentive to anyone else in case it diverted the stream of love and affection which she felt was for her and her alone.

I may well be doing her an injustice, but it is something that even if we were able to discuss, we would never resolve now. I think that the eldest daughter is always in competition with her mother to some extent. I knew at that time that she had the edge on me. She was still good-looking, physically attractive and she understood men. I had none of these qualities, but being at a disadvantage didn't lessen my attempts to share something of dad. It may have made me more bitter that I was unable to succeed, and indeed eventually had to surrender, because when I got the sack from the laundry where I'd been working and mum suggested that I should go into service, I accepted her advice without demur. I could see that this was the answer to the problem that had been obsessing me ever since I had heard mum and dad quarrelling. This was the way to keep the family united.

My first months in service as a kitchen-maid were, without doubt, the most wretched in my life. They were made worse because of my happy home life. Generally speaking, up until then I had enjoyed myself. I had been a somebody. As eldest sister to a large family I had to take on responsibilities which made me, as it were, a second mother to the younger children. Although I didn't like all the things I had to do, I did enjoy the overall feeling of contributing, of being useful and being needed. In service I was the lowest of the low. I wasn't ill-treated but I was ignored, which to me, I think, was worse. I was a no one. It has been suggested to me that this is an experience which upper-class children also have when they go to their public schools. From being important members of their preparatory schools, there they are treated as less than the dust. But they're prepared for this from birth, so it is more easily acceptable to them; also they are not alone, there are other new boys or girls in the same boat with whom they can share feelings. I had no one. I couldn't even tell mum and dad. They might have taken pity on me and told me to leave and go back home which would have upset my plan.

Today of course the pattern of family life is different for ordinary people. Women are considered to be wage earners within the family economic framework. As soon as she can get the children off her hands, and that means out of the house for most of the day, a mother does. The children accept this and rely more on their school, their friends, the television, the pop scene, the coffee bars and discotheques than they do on their parents, so when they finally go away from home, it means little or nothing to them.

I'm glad to say that after a few months, while not accepting it, I grew accustomed to my way of life in service. My break from home became more complete as time went on. At first I would go there for every moment of my time off, but as other interests and excitements entered my life my visits were gradually reduced, and eventually when I went to work in London I went home only once a month. This, I think, was the way my life should have worked out. My ties of home and family were never broken but other events and relationships weakened the bonds. From now on I lived a life in my own right.

A year before I went into service our family economy had taken a change for the better. No longer was dad's working life so erratic as he'd got a permanent job decorating for the Hove Corporation. The money wasn't great but it was steady. Also there were now two of us children earning. Bert was getting seventeen and six a week out of which mum had twelve and six, and I got ten shillings, and kept half a crown. By the time I left home my second brother, John, was contributing to the family kitty, so mum could now plan her life for some time ahead. This reflected in our diet. Dad's favourite meal for instance was a bacon pudding, it now became ours. When finances were uncertain, mum had made it with a bit of bacon in at one end and a strip of bacon rind on the outside to show which end it was; now there was bacon in it for all of us. We got the meat, not just the flavour. It's extraordinary that we children liked dad so much considering the preferential treatment he got. The grocer's list for him was always separate from that of the rest of the family and contained such items as two ounces of butter, an egg, two rashers and half a cup of jam. These were luxuries that we rarely had and we'd sit gazing at him with envy, but it was envy and not jealousy. We realised that dad was the main worker in the family, that he must be fed and kept in good health.

After I'd been away from home for some time and more so when I went to work in London, I was able to observe mum objectively. Her attitude to her children's marriages particularly interested me. She had always gone on about how she wanted to see us all happily married, how she wasn't going to stand in our way, how through her own experience with dad this was the ultimate fulfilment of anyone's life, but when it came to the crunch, and Bert's intended was the first crunch, it was a different matter. He brought her home and probably because I was so like mum, I could sense how she felt. I wasn't sure what emotion it was; it was either grief or rage. To sit there with this woman knowing that she meant more to Bert than she did was almost more than mum could stand, and to listen to her saying what they were going to do together and how she would look after him, and the way she was going to run the home left her seething, not with rage, but with frustration. How could she make this girl see that no matter what she did for Bert she would never be able to look after him half as well as she had herself. What almost made it worse was that she liked the girl and could see that she was right for Bert. It was just that he was the first to be leaving and it was therefore the beginning of the break-up of the home, the thing that mum had had to work so hard to keep together. It had been her whole life, dad and the home. Now I can appreciate her feelings. Although I always said that I wanted my sons to get married early so that I could start leading the life I'd mapped out for myself, when I met their girl friends I was always quite certain that none of them would be able to do half as much for them as I had.

It's interesting that as time went by I, who now felt quite independent of my family and enjoyed this feeling, suddenly found that instead of coming home once a month or sometimes once every two months, and then out of a sense of filial duty, was now visiting them once a week and because I wanted to. It reminds me of that story I've heard since, about the daughter of seventeen who thought her parents ignorant and old-fashioned and then when she was twenty-one was astonished at how much they had learnt over the past four years. Mum continued to infuriate me, but I loved her and I needed her love for me. I needed dad's of course as well, as I had all my life. Now I could tell mum things more. Personal things like about an unhappy love affair. Mine were very volatile affairs. I only had to be going out with a young man for a week or two and I'd think this was for keeps. Then he'd have different ideas and I'd be in the depths of despair. I'd go to mum and she'd put it in the right perspective, the right perspective for me that is. She'd say that he was a stupid boy who didn't recognise a good thing when he was on to it, that I'd be better off without him, that I was much too good for him any-way, and that there were more and bigger fish in the sea than ever came out. All the old clichés, but they were comforting at the time. Not the one about the fish and the sea, because I knew there was a paucity of men as a result of the war. Mum was a great comfort and help to me.

After I got married to Albert, my milkman husband, I would often ask him what he thought of mum when I first took him home. He preserved a discreet silence until one night when we'd both of us had a few drinks, indeed he was more than slightly sloshed, mum's name came up. He lurched back in his chair and said, 'You've always wanted to know, love, what I thought about your mum when we first met. Well, I'll tell you. I'd not been in your house half an hour when I looked at her and then at you and said to myself, "Albert," I said, "it can't be worth it."' Not unnaturally I took umbrage at this. 'Don't mind me,' I said. 'You get it off your chest.' 'Yes I'm going to,' he said. 'You asked for it so you may as well know once and for all. The thing that annoyed me particularly was the way she kept saying, "Margaret will make you a good wife, she's just like me," as if this was some sort of special recommendation. "Not bloody likely she won't be, not if I marry her," I said to myself and you're not, love, you're not.' I think he said this to reassure himself, but he was wrong. I am very much like her.

I remember that first meeting so well. Albert had come home to stay with me. We both of us had a week's holiday. During that week his mother, whom I'd previously met and liked, came down to visit us for the day. Albert's mum was a wonderful woman. She'd been deserted by her husband. He went off and left her with nine children, when the eldest was only fifteen years old, yet she managed to bring them all up herself. Albert was very close to her because her eldest son had died of consumption and the second had gone away from home when he was seventeen, so Albert became the kind of father figure to the family. When he'd seen his mum off at the station after her visit, Albert came back home and took me out for a drink. Over the drink he said, 'If I'd known it was going to upset mum so much, I wouldn't have thought about getting married.' This made me very upset. 'You don't have to, you know. We can call it all off now.' It wasn't a good beginning. Now from having liked his mother I felt hostile towards her. It had really been mum's fault. She should have done her best to put her at her ease, instead of which she seemed almost to go out of her way to disagree with everything she said. They were, of course, complete opposites, but even opposites can be pleasant to each other if they both are prepared to try, at any rate for a day or two. After that I was never able to get on with Albert's mum so well nor she with me. I remember some time later when I was expecting my third child, she came over to see us. Although she had had nine children, she was against large families and really I agreed with her. When we met she looked me up and down and her first words were, 'What's this you've been doing.' I, of course, got livid. 'I don't know what you mean by what have I been doing. It's what your son has done I should have thought!' But of course she knew it was my doing, that women, at any rate by this time, had to take a lead in such matters and that I'd got pregnant because I wanted a girl. I didn't get one.

Fortunately Albert and my dad got on like a house on fire. In all the time they knew each other they never had a cross word.

It's a pity, I think, that Albert hadn't a dad at home. I'm sure I would have got on well with him. I once said this to Albert but he hated his dad and as it started a row between the two of us I never mentioned it again.

From a distance I was able to watch my brothers and sisters growing up. It all seemed a little unfair to me. They got away with murder. For example I had never been allowed out alone at night until I went into service, and then I had to be in at nine-thirty. Yet my younger sister, Pat, was out until nine at the age of twelve with her sweetheart whom she eventually married. By the time she was fourteen she was staying out until after ten and dad would be sent out by mum on his bicycle to scour the streets for her. Pat used to say how awful mum was to her, but she didn't let it deter her. It seems to me that it's the elder children that fight the battles for emancipation with their parents, but only the younger ones reap the benefit. I remember when I was Pat's age saying to mum that she couldn't have much confidence in the way she'd brought us up if she thought all the time that we were liable to go off the straight and narrow. I could have saved my breath. She didn't change as far as I was concerned. Perhaps it was just me she didn't trust. I don't suppose parents change much though. I bet if I'd had a girl I would have behaved the same way that mum did.

In the years between the two wars four of mum's six children got married, and Donald and Elsie grew up. Mum's mother died in 1936, ten years after she had gone to live with her. Mentally she didn't change during the time she was there. She never became violent. Physically she continued to epitomise the sweet old lady, except when she was approached by her imaginary enemies and had to repel them with her hat pin. Until she finally took to her bed, her skin was clear and wrinkle free. She never became scruffy or huddled up, and her hair kept its texture and lovely whiteness. That she was like this says much for the way mum looked after her. Mum refused to let her go into hospital and nursed her until her death. She didn't want to die. She refused to die. It was terrible for mum. Her body literally decomposed before she gave up the struggle.

Albert and I lived in London with our young family. We couldn't visit Hove as often as we'd have liked but I corresponded with mum and there was the feeling that she was always there. When war was again declared she was both angry and worried. This time she knew there would be no escaping involvement for her and her family. Dad wouldn't have to go away but she had three sons who were almost bound to be called up. Her letter writing to me increased with the risk of war and the tone of her letters was such that if determination and will power could have averted a conflict, hers would have.

When war came Albert packed me and the three children off to Hove. We sort of evacuated ourselves from London because my sister, Pat, and her husband invited us to stay with them. It says everything for the kind of nature that she has, that with two young children of her own, we only had one tiff in six months. Pat was, and still is, an amalgam of mum's common sense and dad's good nature. She's not militant or aggressive, she'll always try to do good yet she's not a goody-goody. She's always been 'with it'. She cut her hair when the Eton Crop was all the rage, she learnt all the new dances the moment they came out, and today she keeps pace with the pop scene, yet still retains her dignity. I suppose I ought to have been jealous of her. She was always in demand, she was prettier and more popular than I was. Mum used to say so. 'You'll never get a man. You're too caustic, too critical. No one will marry you, they couldn't bear it. Everyone's got sore points. You look for them and when you've found them you fill them with salt. Why can't you be more like your sister Pat?' Mum could be terrible to me. All right there was probably some truth in what she said, but it might have set me against my sister.

The first thing dad did when war was declared was to dig a large hole in the back garden. Since the air raids didn't begin immediately as he'd expected, he lost interest in it when it had got to about four feet deep. Then one Sunday morning the sirens went. Dad rushed to mum, took her outside, and pushed her in this hole. Being five foot eight, he made her stoop down, put some planks on top of her to protect her from the shrapnel and stood guard over her with the spade on his shoulder like a rifle. Mum, of course, couldn't stand this crouching down for long. 'Let me out,' she called, 'I've got the cramp.' Reluctantly dad obeyed. Aggrieved and dishevelled mum went back into the house and vowed she'd stay there until dad had built a real shelter for her. 'A proper fool you made of me, Harry,' she said. 'Let's hope the neighbours didn't see.' We children have always said it was the only chance he'd ever had of keeping mum down and he was determined to make the most of it.

Donald, her youngest, was the first of mum's children to go to war. He was about twenty at the time and some months back had joined the Territorials as an engineer. I don't think he did it because of any patriotic motives. He was a bit wild at the time like dad was at his age, and enjoyed men's company. It gave him something to do two evenings a week, the parades and drills and of course the drinking afterwards. He got called up a fortnight before war was declared and it wasn't more than a few weeks later that he got embarkation leave before going to France. I went down to see him off. He was so young and frail-looking. I wept buckets. Mum looked very strained. She'd have strangled Hitler there and then if she'd been able to get hold of him. She'd have done worse to him during the days around the evacuation of Dunkirk. Naturally we'd heard nothing from my brother. Then we got a card, 'Safe and sound. Donald.' They were the finest words mum and I had ever had.

My early affinity with Donald when he was a baby had developed into a perfect brother and sister relationship. We both had similar natures. We were extrovert, we didn't conform, we laughed a lot and though also we could be down in the depths, we were never apathetic. He was obviously mum's favourite son. This, I think, was because the passionate relationship between mum and dad had lost some of its fire. They didn't need the outward expression of love so much as the deeper feelings of unity, trust and security, so mum was able to give more affection to her children. She wrote to Donald once, sometimes twice a week, and she was always preparing parcels for him which she sewed up in linen. He was able to say with honesty that her parcels had arrived in perfect condition.

Gradually others of mum's family were caught up in the war effort. Bert went into the Army, John into the Fire Service, and Elsie, the youngest, into the Land Army. Why she chose the Land Army I don't know. We all told her that if she was anything like the rest of the family, she wouldn't enjoy being in the country. She didn't, but she made the best of it. She looked very fetching in her uniform with the green jersey, and apparently the social life of the village of Thakenham in Sussex was at the time of very good quality. There were hundreds of troops stationed around, and the village maidens, who according to Elsie were mostly plain and dumb, suddenly found they were in great demand. Elsie who was bright and attractive had the pick of the bunch. She showed a particular liking for Canadians. They responded. Whether it was because of Elsie's fascination or because their wives and sweethearts were three thousand miles away is a matter for speculation. She got some very nice presents from them. One even gave her a bicycle, I suppose to speed his love even quicker to him. At one time, I think, mum had hopes that Elsie would marry a Canadian. She thought it would be really something to have a daughter out there. She could go and visit her and of course she could have talked about 'My daughter in Canada, you know.' It seems all these Canadians were rich and had ranches, officers and privates as well. As I remarked, 'I know it's a big country but even so there just wouldn't be room for all of them.' Anyway I'm sure mum's glad now like the rest of us, that Elsie didn't marry one.

After six months of the war in Hove, I went back to London. We hadn't had the expected air raids, I was missing Albert and he was missing me. It wasn't long after I'd rejoined him that the bombing started, but somehow it seemed right for us to take our chances and see it out together. When Albert was called up into the RAF in 1941, he was posted to Yorkshire where he saw no enemy action and very few even of our own aircraft. I thought there was no point in myself and the children staying as targets for the Germans, so we rented a house in Hove and moved down there again.

Rationing was now getting difficult. For example we were lucky if we got one egg a week. Dad had the bright idea of keeping chickens. This meant us giving up our chance for an egg a week on the rations in exchange for foodstuff to feed them. We had visions of delicious fresh eggs every day. I don't know where dad got these chickens from, mum reckons it must have been some jungle, because they ate their young. The moment one of them laid an egg they'd all crowd round, peck at the shell until they broke it and then eat the contents. We got so exasperated. We'd sit in the kitchen and the moment we heard a hen clucking because it had laid an egg, we'd rush out to try and save it. We were never successful, so dad decided we'd eat the cannibals. This was some compensation, they were delicious. Dad was so pleased that he bought a dozen cockerels to fatten up for Christmas. We watched them grow. Every time I went round I'd go out and drool over them. They looked pretty disgusting because this lot pecked at each others feathers and so before long they were running around half naked. They used to crow a lot too. Apart from waking mum and dad at the crack of dawn, it was also a pity because it gave someone in the neighbourhood ideas. One morning when dad went out to feed them, he found that three of them were missing. They'd been stolen. One of the neighbours suggested that a fox might have got them. This was a mistake on her part because dad was in one of his very rare rages. He wasn't going to see his Christmas dinner disappear under his very eyes, so every night he brought the remaining nine indoors and put them in the bathroom. This caused a lot of the remaining feathers to fly, and apart from having to catch and carry the birds twice a day, dad also had the job of clearing out the bathroom before mum wanted to go in there. However when Christmas came we all said his efforts had been worth while.

The longer it went on the more mum's fury at the whole business of war increased. Hitler and Mussolini got the main force of it but there was quite a bit left for the government. However much the King and Country needed her sons, mum needed them very much more, and she said so. She was particularly infuriated when dad had to do firewatching. Although he used to grumble about it in front of her, secretly, I think, he enjoyed sitting with his mates over copious cups of tea, smoking and playing cards through the night. Mum and dad had now acquired one of the steel table Morrison shelter things and they slept under this in the sitting-room each night. One night while dad was firewatching, mum climbed up on this table to adjust the blackout. As she was getting down again she slipped and fell, and broke a bone in her leg. Fortunately the neighbours heard her cries and sent round for my sister, Pat, and me. We had the job of getting her to hospital. She wanted none of it and we had to carry her forcibly into the ambulance. She'd never been inside a hospital before, and after a couple of hours it was certain they would never want her in there again. As she was passed from department to department she criticised everything and everybody with bitter invective. She'd always been the one to give orders and she didn't like taking them. Pat and I could see the funny side of it all and were convulsed with mirth. We got some funny looks both from the staff and the other patients. It's become a regular saying between us, 'Haven't laughed so much since the night mum broke her leg.'

It was some time after the war ended before our family was reunited. John was the first out from the Fire Service, then Bert from India, Elsie, and finally Donald, who after Dunkirk had fought backwards and forwards in the desert, then up Italy, and had come through without a scratch. We hadn't seen him for six years and he was very different from the mild, cheeky boy we'd seen off at the station. He soon settled down into a job at the gas works, married and had a baby girl. It was bitterly ironic that he who had survived such a hard fought war, should have lost his life by falling from a roof while at work, less than two years later.

Chapter Eleven

In 1946 dad retired from his job with the Council. He was sixty-four and shouldn't have had to leave for another year, but his health wasn't good and it was felt that it might deteriorate. By now all the children were married and since they were living nearby, mum didn't see the point of having a three-bedroomed council house, so she decided they'd be better off in an old people's council flat. I think she had visions of a cosy little place that could be kept clean with little effort from her. She must have been reading one of those magazines that make everything look and seem so simple but forget that you have to live, cook and sleep in the place, and that things need storing and have to be got at regularly. It was a pity that mum made the decision before the Council sent someone round to coerce them to go. Then wild horses wouldn't have dragged her away. As it was it turned out to be a disappointment to them both. These flats had been built some thirty years back, like a row of terraced houses, one upstairs and one down. Each tenant had his own entrance. There were no bathrooms, no hot water or central heating, and if you had an upstairs flat as mum and dad did, the coal bunker was built into the sitting-room. It may have been logical, based on the assumption that old people couldn't carry their coal upstairs, but it was impractical, dirty and dusty. Mum had hers moved out and bought another which she put at the top of the stairs. This was good for an ordinary sized person's stomach muscles but excluded any possibility of a visit from someone even slightly obese. The rent of course was less and dad had a small pension from the Council, but as mum bitterly complained this did them no good at all because anyone who hadn't a pension got social security. There dad had been working all these years at a low wage because of a pension, when he might just as well have got more and gone on the government when he retired. It didn't make sense to her. I must say it doesn't to me. They both missed their friends and neighbours, who had promised them they would visit them, but they never did. Dad missed his garden, his chickens (he'd managed to persuade them now not to eat their eggs), his pub and the moving around in familiar surroundings. He had lost any purpose in life. We had to watch him getting frailer and frailer, while mum seemed even more energetic than before. She still had a job to do, shopping, cooking and running the flat. She was necessary. Dad felt superfluous. He died six years after they moved into the flat. I think he died in self defence.

He was the kindest and most generous man I have ever met. Yet I was never able to know him as well as I wished. He was reticent. I didn't get near enough to him. He never spoke of the things close to his heart. Perhaps he couldn't. I know that he loved all his children, but I think he loved me in particular. Yet because in our family outward signs of affection were never shown, because mum and dad never kissed us goodnight, because neither of them said how much they loved us, somehow I have never at any time been able to express my love for them. I was with dad on the night he died and I longed to be able to kneel by his bedside and say, 'Dad, thank you for being so good to us, I love you dad.' Every time I tried to I was overcome with embarrassment. I felt even at that time that he would think it wrong for me to try to clothe in words my private feelings.

After dad died, all of us rallied round mum. We thought that to have her children calling on her would be some sort of compensation. It was at first. I'd visit her twice a day and listen while she talked about her life with dad. Not for mum, a veil of silence over the dead. She would relate their lives and relationship together from the time she first met him. I think it was right that she did. The conspiracy of silence that so many relations adopt about the dead doesn't help. It makes it appear as if those that are gone never lived. It was far better to talk about dad, to keep him alive in spirit. After all death is inevitable, it's only the way there that is different. The great thing about mum was that she had no regrets. She didn't keep on about, 'If only I'd done this or done that.' All she wanted to do was relive their lives together. I remember once when Pat and I had been listening to her all afternoon, mum saying as we left, 'Now that I've talked to you both I feel ten years younger.' And as we went down the stairs I said to Pat, 'And we feel ten years older.' Yet we could both see the value it had had for her. It's all very well for me to say that dad died in self defence, that mum dominated and overshadowed him. Perhaps this was what he wanted, someone to make all the decisions. Up to the very end he adored mum and she him. Perhaps towards the end he wanted more quiet, but who are we to say. It's only since he died that mum felt the need to talk about him; while he was there, her life was complete. I feel even today as I listen to her that, though she professes no Christian belief and doesn't go to church she feels dad is still with her and is sure she is going to meet him in the hereafter.

For the next fifteen years mum seemed to grow even more energetic. When she was well over eighty she thought nothing of walking from Hove to Brighton and back. Often she'd start by waiting for a bus but if one didn't come within a minute, she'd make an expression of disgust and decide to walk. She was always an impatient woman. The thing that annoyed me, and I think my brothers and sisters, was that mum refused to allow us to compensate for dad. We tried so hard, visiting her, talking and listening to her, taking her flowers, chocolates and drink, but she'd always got her grumbles about how lonely she was. I used to say how fortunate she was to have five of us children and her grandchildren going so regularly to see her. She'd just grunt. Then I'd compare her lot with that of so many of the other old people who lived around her, many of whom hadn't got anybody to care for them. 'What have they got to do with me?' she'd reply. What can you say to a woman like that? Only agree with her that contemplating other people's miseries doesn't help you to bear your own. Mum resented that she was incidental in our lives; with dad she had been the only one.

That of course didn't help us. Anyone who makes a sacrifice wants either signs of gratitude or spoken thanks for doing it. We didn't get either. When I told mum she ought to show gratitude, she just said, 'Wait till it happens to you,' in a hollow sort of voice. 'If Albert were to die before me,' I said, 'I'd have no one. My sons are scattered and I have no daughters. I wouldn't have as good a life as you're having.' 'Now don't start being jealous,' she replied. 'You should have thought of this before you gave up having a proper family.' What could you say? Even I was speechless.

Some five years ago the Council decided to modernise the flats where mum lives by adding bathrooms. This gave the residents many days of excitement. Enormous cranes arrived in the street and lifted the units over the roofs of the homes. Soon they all had baths, sink units and hot water. The rents rose of course, but since all of them were on Public Assistance no one noticed the difference there. Mind you they weren't all happy with what they got for nothing. One old lady assured me that she'd managed perfectly well all her life without having a bath. She'd never missed it. She didn't hold with all this washing of the skin. 'It weakens it,' she said. Another couple had the coal bunker moved into the bathroom. 'We shan't use the bath and it'll give us more space in the sitting-room,' they said. Two old ladies tried one straight away and neither of them could get out, despite the fact that a pole had been fixed to the side of the bath for them to hold on to. 'Would have perished with the cold if our neighbours hadn't come and helped us out,' they both said.

Mum revelled in it at first, but eventually even she hadn't the strength to get herself out. When Pat and I heard about this we offered to come in and bath her. She wouldn't hear of her children seeing her in the nude. She got a stranger in from the Council to do it, twice a week. When she refused us I said, 'It's the first time I've ever known you to be modest about something, mum.' She didn't like that.

I know I've said this before, but I believe that some of the blame for the plight of old people (and as most of them like mum don't suffer in silence, it's visited on the friends and relatives who go to see them) lies with the Town Councils. They should not build roads of houses and flats just for old people. They should not move them from their familiar surroundings where they've been a part of a community made up of all ages and interests. They should look at 'our street' as I've tried to show it, and encourage the kind of spirit which was so much alive there when we were growing up. Where unostentatious good neighbourliness abounded. I don't think that people today have really changed. Instead of the do-gooders whom we could then ignore, we have a social system run by faceless wonders. We've become a nation of form-fillers. I'm not saying that social service is wrong: it's too clinically administered. Take the road where mum and dad went to live. If a clerk working for the council gets a letter from there he says, 'Oh yes, that's the old people's road.' They're bracketed, segregated. They are no longer Mr and Mrs Smith with a circle of friends and neighbours. They're Old Mr and Mrs Smith on the pension and getting National Assistance. They are also now referred to as the Town's Senior Citizens, which is a nonsense because there aren't any Junior or Middle-aged citizens. Thank God we haven't stooped to calling ourselves citizens yet; brothers is bad enough among men who aren't related.

Another thing about mum's road was that it was a cul-de-sac. You can understand the thinking of the planners, 'It will be nice and quiet for them.' But old people don't want that sort of quiet, and in this road it was the quietness of the grave because some joker, to underline the time of life of the people living in it, sited a mortuary at the end. Death is just around the corner! To make sure that no one lived in ignorance of the fact they put a notice up: MORTUARY, in nice big letters.

Fortunately most of them who live there are able to laugh at it. I remember once I hadn't been to see mum for a day or two and when I called she adopted the expression of a martyr. I enquired what the matter was. 'I don't feel right,' she said. 'Perhaps we'd better get the doctor in. Where's the pain?' I asked. 'Oh I'm not in pain,' she said quickly. 'It's just that I don't feel as if I'm long for this world.' She pulled the sort of face that didn't look as though she was either. 'I'm not grumbling of course. I've had a good life, I know. There's no use me grumbling.' But she was grumbling and it infuriated me. 'Look, mum,' I said, 'if that's how you feel, why don't you walk quietly up to the mortuary and lie down there? It'll save us all a lot of trouble.' Give mum her due, she roared with laughter and soon forgot her misery.

A thing that has irritated mum for a long time is the business about the money for her funeral. Like other people in our street mum took out an insurance for twenty pounds, which she finished paying long ago. Just after dad died, and he had a similar policy, she decided that twenty pounds wouldn't be enough, so she contributed a shilling a week to allow for another ten pounds. Well, that was twenty years ago and she knows that she's paid out much more than will ever come back, and it makes her mad. She can't see that the insurance company took a risk at the time.

Last year, in 1971, when she was ninety it became obvious that mum couldn't go on looking after herself. My sister, Pat, volunteered to have her to live with her husband and herself. I don't need to say what I think of her for doing this. I can say that it wouldn't have done for mum and me to live together now. We should quarrel all the time. It has been possible for me to help in certain ways. I visit her regularly, we chat and play cards together, and because I now have a bit of money I can buy her things which make life more enjoyable. She's got a colour television, a swivel chair, so that when we're sitting in the room with her she can quickly turn round and face whoever's talking, and of course I always see that she has what drink she wants. She enjoys her whisky but perhaps even more her three bottles of barley wine a day. If anybody writes to tell me it isn't good for her, I shall set mum on to them. As she says, 'If I care to die of drink at ninety-one it's my own business.' But where she is lucky is that she is still able to occupy herself. She reads voraciously; despite two cataract operations, her sight is excellent. She no longer reads as deeply as she did. She likes novels now and gets through about three a week. She enjoys crocheting and she makes some very beautiful things. Her hearing isn't quite what it was; she says she's deaf, but if you criticise her or offer her a drink she's very quick to respond. None of these things though compensate for the fact that she can't have company whenever she wants it. Nor do they stop her looking for it when she has a mind to. Often if she hears voices below she'll make her way downstairs and burst into the room and say, 'You all seem to be enjoying yourselves and having a good time down here—why didn't you ask me to join you?' Then she'll take over the conversation, which generally means a diatribe against the lot of the old in general and hers in particular. Once she's down it's difficult to get her upstairs again, not only because sometimes she doesn't want to go but because the only disability she suffers from is that her legs are weak. This causes her great feelings of frustration. It has taken from her her independence. It irks her to ask for help. It also irks me that she is unable to accept it graciously and I tell her so. 'You wait till you're as helpless as I am. You'll feel the same way as I do,' is the only reply I ever get.

Mum doesn't fear death and talks about it philosophically and sometimes jocularly. 'I know you think I'm a nuisance to you but I'm not dying just to please my relations.' She may not be having a hilarious life here below but as she says she can't be sure that the next one will be as good. She talks about euthanasia but is dead set against it, 'whether it's private or on the health service.' Although as I've said she holds no religious beliefs, she's certain she will see dad again and that she'll be able to keep an eye on all of her family.

I have been so pleased with the way she has accepted the success that I have had late in my life. She is interested in everything I do and lives vicariously through me. Secretly, I think, she believes that given my opportunities she would have been able to have done the same. I know she would.

This book started by being the most difficult I have written. I kept thinking, I can't say this, I mustn't say that, I must get the family's agreement for the other thing. Then I also said to myself, 'What will people think of you if you say that?' If I'd applied these brakes or cautions on what I wanted to write, the book would have been anaemic. So with no apologies to anyone I decided to tell the truth as I saw it. It's probably not the truth as mum sees herself or as the others who have known her think of mum, but it is the way I have observed her and it's my interpretation of her behaviour before I was born. Much of my comment on her has been based on the fact that mum and I are so very much alike and that our lives have both been conditioned by having been in domestic service.